Praise for *Confronting P*

"Donald Trump is a bully. His political power, his popularity with one segment of the American people and the dread he inspires in the rest, and his ascent from sleazeball entrepreneur to President of the United States, are all the fruits of a concerted campaign of intimidation and threat. Today, bullying is less a phenomenon of the schoolyard than of the corporate boardroom and workplace; and Donald Trump, the CEO folk hero, has taken it from there and made it into the central principle of American politics, society, and culture. In this book, Roddey Reid brings us the crucial missing piece of the puzzle of Trump: the way that his fear tactics have created a poisonous structure of feeling that is more deadly than any mere ideology."

— Steve Shaviro, DeRoy Professor of English, Wayne State University

"Deeply researched, conceptually sophisticated, and engagingly written, Roddey Reid's excellent new book makes an indispensable contribution. If you want to understand the current moment of Trump in historical perspective--and if, indeed, you care about the future of the USA--you will find Reid's work of great value. His outlook is always realistic, and often grimly so, but never without hope."

— Carl Freedman, author of *The Age of Nixon*

"Roddey Reid's *Confronting Political Intimidation* is an insightful diagnosis of how we got here, and a potent toolkit to secure a more hopeful future. Reid pulls together a wide range of under-examined material from corporate culture and popular media to source the dark currents now surging through American politics, and finds a fresh vocabulary for democratic renewal."

— Christopher Brown, World Fantasy Award nominee and author of *Tropic of Kansas: A Novel*

"Roddey Reid shows that Trump mastered, but did not originate, the hyper-tough entrepreneurial bully we see today. His book offers a convincing and important study of bullying as the link between austerity, hyper-wealth, and reactionary populism, and forces us to look again at the fabric of our everyday social relations and political choices. To begin to imagine a different kind of politics, to conceive of a more compassionate and knowledgeable society, and to put these goals in practice before it is too late, we need this book."

— Jody Berland, author of *North of Empire: Essays on the Cultural Technologies of Space*

"Reid highlights in this slim volume the ways in which Trump's behavior, and more importantly its resonance with American voters, is less the product of a personality disorder than an expression of the culture of bullying that has become prevalent in business, politics, and media since the days of the Carter stagflation. His nuanced but incisive analysis brings home the dangers posed by this sharp right-wing turn to American institutions and the need to confront it not with better electoral politicking but a deeper participatory democratic and more egalitarian socio-economic vision."

— Gershon Shafir, author of *A Half Century of Occupation: Israel, Palestine, and the World's Most Intractable Conflict*

"Donald Trump has withered himself into an orbit of four basic cravings: maniacal lying (its gravitational influences infect the orbits of the other three), greed, revenge, and his hatching of apparitions, which lure society into feckless vintages of disintegration yet to be named: Roddey Reid, like a 21st century Kepler, traces the sources of these orbits and their vapors, which have already wobbled into the resetting of the Doomsday Clock."

— David Matlin, novelist & essayist; author of *Prisons inside the New America: From Vernooykill Creek to Abu Ghraib*

"If you have found yourself wondering how the President suddenly morphed from the commander-in-chief to the bully-in-chief, this is the book for you. The short answer: it wasn't so sudden. Reid expertly shows how the Trump phenomenon is the culmination of a decades-long history of transformations affecting not only national political discourse but rooted as well in arenas as diverse and pervasive as workplace culture, the neoliberal spirit of capitalism, and the culture of insecurity in the age of limitless war. Trump did not invent this "culture of fear and intimidation." His innovation is to have personified it, channeling its violence toward ever balder and harsher expressions. *Confronting Political Intimidation* is a wake-up call and a call to action in the name of a livable – and shareable – future."

— Brian Massumi, author of *Ontopower: War, Powers, and the State of Exception* and *The Power at the End of the Economy*

To Nicole —
A small contribution to seeing
ourselves through the present
moment towards a better future.
Roddey
Aug 13, 2018

Confronting Political Intimidation and Public Bullying

A Citizen's Handbook for the Trump Era and Beyond

Roddey Reid

My point is not that everything is bad, but that everything is dangerous, which is not the same as bad. If everything is dangerous, then we always have something to do.

Michel Foucault

That's why this moment in history is so important. That's why this group is so important. That's why every one of the people out here is so important. The real question on the line today is, "Can democracy survive this? Can democracy fight back?" ... Our only chance now, really—it's us. That's what we are down to here.

Sen. Elizabeth Warren at Joyous Persistence Event, June 1, 2017[1]

Table of Contents

PREFACE Our Transformed National Life   **10**

**CHAPTER ONE Political Violence, or They Meant
What They Said**   **17**
    Traumatic Lessons: CEO Trump's Hostile Takeover   *17*
    Looking Back: They Meant It   *23*
    9/11, the Iraq Invasion, and the War on Terror   *25*
    *New York City as Laboratory of Intimidation and
Fear*   *28*

**CHAPTER TWO Intimidation and Bullying in the
Wider Culture: The Workplace and the Media**   **31**
    Harsh Climate   *32*
    *Ground Zero: Financial and Managerial Revolution
in the Workplace*   *33*
    The Bullying Boss   *36*
    Short-Term Greed, Long-Term Insecurity   *39*
    The Media Sphere   *40*
    Reality TV and Social Media   *42*

**CHAPTER THREE Enter Trump: The Tyrannical CEO
and White Entrepreneur as Capitalist Folk Hero**   **45**
    The Question   *45*
    Trump the Entrepreneur   *47*
    *Trump's Negative Identity Politics: From Cold War
Smearing to Entrepreneurial Bullying*   *49*
    The Defiant White Man: The Method is the Message   *53*
    Government as Family Business   *56*
    The Political Synergy of Trump's Multiple Identities   *58*
    *After Trump: Entrepreneurialism and Authoritarian
Political Rule*   *59*

CHAPTER FOUR Political Thuggery and Party Identities   **60**
    A Restructured Democratic Party and Its Cautious Strategies   *60*
    The Advent of Obama and the Rise of the Tea Party   *63*
    2010: Demobilizing Democrats   *65*
    Party Loyalty, Social Identity, and Cultures of Governing   *67*
    Donald Trump's Identity and Aggression: He Meant What He Said   *73*

CHAPTER FIVE Playing for Keeps: The 2016 Elections   **75**
    The Abusive Entrepreneur Enters Politics   *75*
    Hillary Clinton's Unflinching Campaign   *76*

CHAPTER SIX Learning from the Dynamics of Political Intimidation and Bullying   **82**
    Preemptive Strike: Creating Public Facts on the Ground   *82*
    Public Bullying   *84*
    The Politics of Destruction   *86*
    Snares and Traps: Denial   *89*
    Snares and Traps: Blind Revenge   *91*
    Snares and Traps: Nostalgia for the Theater of Moral Shaming   *92*
    Snares and Traps: Media Frenzies   *93*

CONCLUSION Renewing Politics   **97**
    On Our Own   *97*
    Rewriting the Political Script   *99*

About the Author   **103**
NOTES   **104**

PREFACE

Our Transformed National Life

> Have fear-producing mechanisms become so pervasive and invasive that we can no longer separate ourselves from our fear? If they have, is fear still fundamentally an emotion, a personal experience, or is it part of what constitutes the collective ground of possible experience?
>
> Brian Massumi, *The Politics of Everyday Fear*[2]

This is an essay on how political intimidation and public bullying have transformed national life in the United States over the last thirty years and how this harsh environment constitutes a direct challenge to citizens and residents, especially those seeking to engage in activism and party politics now and in the years to come.[3] It was prompted by Donald Trump's ascent to the White House but its roots go back to essays I wrote at the close of the George W. Bush years and beginning of the Obama era (2008-09) after living for more than seven years under the War on Terror and cycles of economic bubbles and busts that hurt many and benefitted the privileged few.

Since the kick-off in 2015 of the last presidential campaign, a climate of fear and intimidation has dominated national life in the United States to a degree rarely seen before, poisoning our politics and reaching into our very relationships with friends, co-workers, and neighbors.

This book is about how this came to be, how we can see ourselves through it, but also why it is not likely to go away anytime soon.

Trump's successful candidacy represents the mainstreaming and legitimization of violent forces and political tactics that preceded his election and will endure even after he has left office. He has unleashed frightening public dynamics that have been slowly building for some time and inflaming public life. At the core of this political history is a wider U.S. public culture of intimidation and bullying. This culture emerged in its current form in the workplace, media, and the political arena, when globalization first began and the economy underwent financialization as it fell under the sway of Wall Street and the banking sector in the early 1980s.

It is not by chance that we have today an openly violent president who is also an abusive CEO, freewheeling entrepreneur, and Internet troll. American businesses may be centers of innovation, but they are not leaders in promoting democratic values and respectful citizenship. Trump's powerful melding of racist and misogynistic content with his aggressive entrepreneurialism and management style was the hallmark of his campaign. His unabashed probusiness stance and belligerent sense of political entitlement, both domestically and internationally, are what connects Trumpism to the Republican Party. It is a peculiarly American version of populism that sets it off as a political movement from most contemporary right-wing populisms in other countries.

Trump's populist genius has been at once to personify all that unfettered capitalism promises and to lead a revolt against all its disappointments in the name of those very same promises.4 However, what Trumpism *does* share with these movements is its stated nationalist position in favor of closing borders and deporting immigrants, preserving some form of social insurance for deserving citizens, preventing the offshoring of factories and jobs, adopting protectionist measures, and rebuilding declining economic infrastructure. It is an America-first free-market populist ideology of sorts, which is hostile to globalization and is far more popular with his followers than with the Republican establishment.

In my view, the conservative cult of individual success and fulfillment wedded to aggressive entrepreneurship, unregulated markets, and small government is alive and well. Combined with the promotion of the firm as a model of political rule, it constitutes a political current that feeds Trump's violent white nationalism and much of the Republican agenda, and will nourish other right-wing politicians and programs in the foreseeable future. Intimidation and fear-mongering, now amplified by the endless opportunities for cyberbullying afforded by social media, have become part of the very substance of the new regime's politics.

These are all deeply compelling social and psychological aspects of contemporary culture that are driving our political life. In this I depart from some progressive commentators who see U.S. conservatism as an ideologically bankrupt movement and thus a spent political force, with Trump's victory representing not only this movement's climax but also its death throe. On the contrary, I want to argue that these currents have created a pervasive right-wing public culture of intimidation that will outlast the current administration. It is no transient phenomenon. This culture of bullying and fear has succeeded in linking some of our most subjective, individual experiences with those of collective life itself.

My central thesis about political violence and bullying and their roots in the wider contemporary culture has received surprisingly little sustained attention by journalists and pundits. This short book fills that breach. By placing Trump's actions and those of his Republican allies in a larger social and political context, the goal in writing a handbook is to offer citizens and residents a way to understand Trump and negotiate the current climate of intimidation his surprise victory has deepened. For as Elizabeth Warren reminded us, "Our only chance now, really, is us." It's about shedding light on the dark side of contemporary politics in order to see beyond it.

My hope is that a clear picture will help diminish the terror of the present moment and encourage a lucid and steadfast activism. Writing about another source of considerable collective anxiety, the struggle against global warming, geographer Matthew Sparke makes this point eloquently: "False hopes and groundless fears can be of dreadful deadly consequences. And yet justified fears when combined with sensible hopes can open new possibilities and thereby help mobilize change for the better."[5] In the end, it is all about being effective, as the Women's March and the activism of Black Lives Matter, Swing Left, and Indivisible's 6,000 chapters since Trump's inauguration have taught us.

Broaching the question of political violence and bullying is no simple task, for the right has sequestered and made their own the discourses of fear and intimidation and wielded them to control the public. Trump and the Republicans have emboldened the most extreme elements of our society including white supremacists and the Internet-based alt.right, some of whose leaders such as Steve Bannon and Sebastian Gorka have entered the White House. Fear and dread proliferate and paralyze; at their most powerful they even shape people's responses, provoking blind panic and, in some cases, violence. My hope is that by connecting the many dots of events that we have witnessed and remember, the book will serve as an actual guide for those working to oppose the right-wing juggernaut in Washington to the strategies and dynamics of contemporary political intimidation and bullying: the dangers they present, the snares and traps that envelop their targets, and the lessons to be learned.

We progressives and liberals[6] have yet to integrate into our thinking and strategies this dark political information (and just why it is so difficult for Democratic Party leaders to do so is a subject I also explore). Until we do, we will be taken by "surprise" again and again by the lengths to which the new regime will go to achieve its goals and how such political violence and bullying can create its own momentum, which under the right circumstances can even rewrite the very script of how politics in a democracy is conducted. What follows is a small attempt to expand the resistance's powers of anticipation and counteraction to the current right-wing onslaught.

The first five chapters lay the groundwork for the lessons offered in Chapter Six and the Conclusion. Chapter One is an overview that glances back in time at the roots of current forms of political intimidation. The story of the how the wider culture coarsened and then enabled right-wing political agendas and extremely aggressive political tactics is then pursued in Chapter Two, which focuses on the revolution in acceptable public behavior and speech that took place in the workplace and media. Chapter Three follows up by outlining how an abusive boss like Donald Trump could flourish and become a potent political force in this new environment. Chapters Four and Five review the long history of political violence and electoral skullduggery and weak Democratic responses to it; they bring that history up to the 2016 elections and the present, in terms of Republicans' and Democrats' party identities, social makeup, practices of political loyalty, and conceptions of government.

Chapter Six proposes a distillation of the dynamics of public intimidation and political bullying encountered in the preceding chapters and considers what we can learn from them as we oppose the conservative counter-revolution in Washington through forms of activism and party politics in a resolutely hostile political climate. Finally, the Conclusion looks forward to how citizens can convert these lessons into clear-eyed and effective activism.

Portions of Chapters One and Two draw on early articles I published in the U.S, Canada, and France on public cultures of intimidation and bullying: "Bullying in U.S. Public Culture: or, Gothic Terror in the Full Light of Day," *TOPIA: Canadian Journal of Cultural Studies* (Fall 2008): 129-49; "La culture d'intimidation aux Etats-Unis," *Esprit* (août-septembre 2009): 50-68; "The American Culture of Public Bullying," *Black Renaissance Noire* 9.2-3 (Fall-Winter 2009-10): 174-87; and "Affect, Trauma, and Daily Life: Transatlantic Legal and Medical Responses to Bullying and Intimidation," in *Science & Emotions after 1945: A Transatlantic Perspective*, ed. Frank Biess and Daniel Gross (Chicago, 2014), 265-86. A brief version of Chapter Three was first posted to my personal blog, "UnSafe Thoughts," in July 2016, and then published as "Trump as Capitalist Folk Hero, or The Rise of the White Entrepreneur as Political Bully," *Black Renaissance Noire* 16.2 (Fall 2016): 92-95. Chapters Four and Five are greatly revamped and expanded versions of postings to my blog in March 2017.

The urgent nature of *Confronting Political Intimidation* led me to choose initially the unusual route of electronic self-publishing in order to take advantage of the greater affordability, speed, and accessibility it possesses over the slower print venues of academic and commercial publishers. For most presses, electronic publishing is only an appendage of traditional print publishing, and still involves a lengthy vetting and production process. As an emeritus professor, professional and institutional validation by academic and commercial print venues is less important to me than the rapid dissemination of ideas at a reasonable price to engaged citizens and residents facing a forbidding political environment in the context of a national crisis.

This is a single-authored book in the new age of crowd-sourcing but it does depend on the work of many other researchers, writers, journalists, activists, artists, and scholars. Their important work is referenced in the endnotes with available URLs. The entire book can be read without consulting any notes, but they do provide interested readers additional details and more in-depth analysis of particular points as well as suggestions for further reading.

Sincere thanks go to colleagues, friends, and family who gave input and encouragement concerning many of the ideas and sections of this short volume: Marcel Hénaff gave initial impetus to my research, when he invited me in February 2008 to give a lecture in his graduate seminar in political theory on the politics of fear, terrorism, and democracy at the University of California San Diego. Gershon Shafir, David Matlin, and Steve Shaviro saw the value of my writing through its many iterations, sometimes before I did. My thinking acquired public legs thanks to three editors, who welcomed the wide-ranging experimental nature of my early essays that didn't fit easily in standard academic journals: Jody Berland of *TOPIA: Canadian Journal of Cultural Studies*, Olivier Mongin of *Esprit*, and Quincy Troupe of *Black Renaissance Noire*. Lori Boatright, Lisa Cartwright, John Erni, Ari Heinrich, Jerry Karabel, Ping-hui Liao, Isaac Martin, Brian Massumi, Jeffrey Minson, Chris Newfield, Toru Tani, Yu Tani, Akos Rona-Tas, Dan Selden, Lesley Stern, Shankar Subramaniam, and Charles Thorpe gave input from nearby and afar. I owe Martha Rosler the phrase "incompetent authoritarian" to describe Donald Trump's performance since assuming office.

Joyce Clements shared with me her experience as an editor, Flora Bloom and Liz Maruska have been warmly enthusiastic, and Lucy Reid communicated wisdom and skepticism from the perspective of a former business consultant and senior executive. May Joseph introduced me to the brave new world of e-book self-publishing. Pam Rosenthal and Michael Rosenthal of P&M Editorial Services provided expert copywriting and formatting assistance. Finally, Lisa Bloom was a steadying presence intellectual and otherwise through the ups and downs of writing in politically difficult times without which this book would not have seen the light of day.

Net proceeds from sales will go to Indivisible National of IndivisibleGuide.com.

Berkeley and New York
August 31, 2017

CHAPTER ONE

Political Violence, or They Meant What They Said

Traumatic Lessons: CEO Trump's Hostile Takeover

Make no mistake about it. Seven months on, we are still in the midst of a far-right counterrevolution in Washington to remake the federal government as we've known it for the last eighty years. Even if it shows signs of faltering and doesn't achieve some of its most ambitious goals, it will remain a powerful political force to be reckoned with and, like a wounded beast, is no less dangerous than before.

Those who naively hoped that Trump would "mature" and "grow" into the office under the pressures of daily governance and that he would delegate policymaking to experienced Beltway politicians and experts now know better. Trump, ever the aggressive entrepreneur and domineering boss, from day one in the White House has treated the federal government like a privately held company of which he is sole owner and CEO, thus lending a new twist to the expression "privatization." We are living the aftermath of a hostile takeover of the federal government by a corporate raider who is now bent on restructuring his latest acquisition.

Trump's ascent to the White House is just the latest stage and logical next step in the long career of a mogul whose family businesses have profited from close relationships with government officials, especially in the form of public contracts, building code variances, and extravagant tax breaks on real estate deals. As the late investigative *Village Voice* reporter Wayne Barrett wrote of Trump's candidacy, "So it shouldn't surprise that Donald now wants to be the state itself, the grand culmination of the family's business plan, and a merger of public and private power with disturbing precedents."7

Since Trump assumed office, he has pursued the same shock and awe tactics he displayed during his campaign, as he and his Republican allies work doggedly to dismantle or defund immigration policies, the Affordable Care Act, global warming agreements, the Dodd-Frank financial safeguards, public education, consumer protections, and net neutrality. Their shared goal is to undo the legacies of the New Deal and Civil Rights eras while he, Trump, seeks to impose his white nationalist political agenda and highly personalized form of authoritarian rule.[8] If anything, the pressures of governing have stimulated Trump's violent, arbitrary nature, not restrained it.

Others, who thought that contradictions or "disjunction" between Trump's stated positions and the agenda of congressional Republicans would restrict the new administration's ability to enact radical change, failed to take into account what they both share in the short term: the violent desire to preemptively wreck past policies during the narrow window of opportunity afforded by Republican control of the executive and legislative branches. It amounted to nothing less than a bid to "create facts on the ground" that recast the very purpose and form of government and citizens' and residents' relationship with the state and public services.[9] It appeared that resolving long-term policy disagreements could wait until presumably a changed federal government and a new political landscape emerged from the wreckage. Such were and still are their desire and goal.

Trump's raw persona operated as a mobilizing force for populist anger and radical Republican anti-government rage, but the aura of power and invincibility that in January 2017 seemed poised to sweep everything before it has begun to lessen. The much-feared international tide of right-wing populism that was set to unfurl in Europe in the wake of Brexit and Trump's victory appears to have receded for now, with electoral setbacks in Austria, the Netherlands, France, and Great Britain even as the enabling social conditions haven't changed. Seven months later, the complex machinery of government, the intricacies of foreign policy, the implacable hostility of the intelligence agencies, fierce public opposition, Republican missteps, and Trump's chaotic family-business management style seem to have slowed the implementation of some of their most radical initiatives.

Every day, it becomes clearer that Trump is no longer in his natural element of the New York business world of commercial real estate. His rough-and-ready entrepreneurialism that served him so well in his business deals and later allowed him to outmaneuver the smug establishments of both parties and bypass hostile media outlets via his Twitter account has not been as effective in Washington. This would seem to be especially true in military and foreign affairs, where the consequences of his actions are so much more immediate and thus subjected to a level of scrutiny that even he, the celebrity CEO, has not quite encountered before. Yet here, too, as in other matters, the greater the scrutiny, the greater defiance, and the more reckless Trump becomes, as the escalating apocalyptic military threats against North Korea as I write make more than clear. He has no effective handlers either domestically or internationally.

More and more we are left with the impression of an incompetent authoritarian who is prisoner of his impulsive personality and unable to develop effective political strategies with Congress. But it would be a mistake to ignore the violent forces and tactics that have carried Trump to the White House and to over-personalize what are deep political changes in our culture, as media outlets seem to be doing. In fact the current media feeding frenzy over investigations into possible Trump collusion with Russian meddling in the election and his murky business dealings may be already generating a surge in loyalty among some his supporters not unlike the backlash against the media's obsessively negative coverage of Trump during the fall 2016 campaign.[10]

We still face wily and remorseless opponents who are quick to resort to tried-and-true tactics of political intimidation. And currently, they are using their control of federal agencies to sabotage Obamacare and carry out their right-wing agenda, and are quietly proceeding to fill over one hundred and twenty vacant Federal judgeships with young, far-right nominees, who once appointed will be in a position to provide for decades to come legal cover for extremist policies. As Naomi Klein is careful to remind us, they are even happy to propose deliberately flawed policies, whose failure will only create worse crises for them to exploit in order to push through their agenda. [11] For them, chaos is an opportunity rather than a political threat or sign of weakness. Only time and the strength of our resistance will tell.

Public reaction to the new regime's early steps has been swift and massive and enjoyed some success thanks in part to a skeptical judiciary. But as liberals, progressives, and other concerned citizens and residents pursue mobilization against the new occupant of the White House, there are lessons to be drawn from his unprecedented acts of personal abuse of rivals, including threats to incarcerate and assassinate his opponent in the general election, and from the acts of political skullduggery that benefitted his campaign, such as the hacking of Democratic leaders' email accounts and the active interference by the then FBI Director James Comey.

At this juncture, then, it may be particularly helpful to revisit the recent U.S. history of political intimidation and violence and Democratic Party responses to them. This will perhaps allow us to gain a better understanding of the current political crisis and especially of the obstacles that people face in galvanizing a Democratic Party establishment that heretofore has shown reluctance to openly mobilize its voters and aggressively and publicly confront long-standing Republican tactics. Trump has now combined these tactics with his own rough brand of political intimidation, bullying, and fear-mongering, lending them a truly psychological and affective dimension that perhaps they didn't quite have before. The roots of this violent political history and of its role in the current crisis go back many years, and they will continue to shape national life long after the Trump administration and the current Republican majorities in Congress are gone.

The 2016 elections can be seen as the expression of voters' fears and grievances, stemming from the experience of living under a destructive market economy including contending with stagnant household wages since the 1970s and fifteen years of the War on Terror. Moreover, the campaign took place in a public climate of uncontrolled violence as the United States witnessed acts of domestic terrorism and mass shootings, brutal treatment by private security contractors of Native American protestors at Standing Rock, North Dakota, and a wave of video recordings of unprovoked police killings of African-American men. Crucially, the primaries and general election were also a traumatic lesson to forgetful Democratic politicians of the power of right-wing intimidation and violence to affect the outcome of election campaigns. They were a reminder that threats and fear-mongering are not occasional excesses of contemporary right-wing politics and policies but an integral part of them.[12]

Arguably, this violence has been there all along, woven into the fabric of cruel Republican-sponsored legislation that seeks to punish citizens and residents by denying them access to basic healthcare and reproductive medicine, workplace and consumer protections, unemployment compensation, a working wage, and a secure retirement. It is there, too, in his cabinet appointees, whose personal fortunes derive from harm knowingly done to vulnerable populations.[13] Perhaps more important, the advent of Donald Trump has highlighted an underappreciated aspect of violent politics: its transformative power. It doesn't leave the political field as it found it. Not only can smears, physical threats, and skullduggery paralyze and defeat opponents, but they can also legitimize the most authoritarian politics and energize the movement or party that deploys them, be it through political speeches, tweets, rallies, or protests. Right-wing politicians and their followers now revel in intimidating and threatening others, glory in it, and find each other and bond through it, even forge a new group identity by means of it.

For many supporters Trump's violence is the very measure of his liberty and credibility. Perhaps even more than the fulfillment of any one of his electoral promises or policies. It is striking that Trump's verbal intimidation and threats against immigrants, the news media, etc. no longer put off establishment conservatives but rather draw them in; they have fallen behind him, not the reverse. If his steady approval ratings among Republicans since the failure to pass Trumpcare and his later pronouncements expressing sympathy for white supremacists who marched in Charottesville, Virginia are any indication, his violent behavior may even substitute for the traditional concrete fulfillment of campaign pledges as the measure of political success. [14]

With Trump, not only has "privatization" of the public weal reached its term. So has the process of "de-democratization," whereby, according to political philosopher Wendy Brown, the positive protocols of business management have migrated to the political arena, thanks in particular to the ongoing privatization of public services. There it has reformulated democracy as a form of corporate governance (in which citizen participation is understood to involve efficient collaboration, partnership, consensus, and problem-solving but under the authoritarian rule of managers) and substituted market metrics for effective political representation, economic redistribution, and social justice as the measure of political achievement.[15]

In the new administration it would appear that corporate management as a model of government has now taken an authoritarian, negative turn that cares little for participation or efficiency at all. And since his election, Trump appears to want to replace citizens' and even public servants' loyalty to the institutions of national government and the rule of law with deference to his defiant CEO-presidential will. The firing of FBI Director James Comey in May 2017 for refusing to profess personal loyalty to him and halt the investigation into former National Security Advisor Michael Flynn's Russian contacts made this clear to one and all, especially within government. And as rumors swirled about the possible firing of Special Counsel Robert Mueller and Attorney General Jeff

Sessions, Trump dropped hints that he has even the right to pardon himself.

This is all vital information that we need to incorporate into our political thinking and strategies, something that has proved especially difficult for Democratic Party leaders (see Chapters Four and Five). Otherwise we will be caught unawares time and time again by the relentlessness of the GOP's violent tactics. I argue that such violence can even recast the very rules by which we do politics. What follows is a small contribution to increasing the resistance's ability to anticipate reactions to its efforts to counter the Republican juggernaut through activism and party politics.

Looking Back: They Meant It

Long ago, we should have seen it coming. It's not like there wasn't ample warning. But few of us wanted to believe them— that they meant what they said. So much macho bluster. Strutting around, talking tough. But following close behind came the actions: fire-bombings of abortion clinics, serial capital executions, gay bashings. Not to mention the "three-strikes" laws and mandatory sentencing that sent Blacks and Latinos off to long prison terms for petty drug offenses and tripled the U.S. prison population within twenty years. As a consequence, a racial caste system recalling the worst aspects of Jim Crow has emerged under the criminal justice system's guise of color-blindness. Next to come in for brutal treatment were the schools and workplaces, from the presence of police in hallways and zero-tolerance drug tests to factory closings and the downsizing of middle management to the cutting and privatization of public services and government programs. Even the Post Office was reorganized to resemble a for-profit enterprise; it also became a symbol of workplace violence. 16

In the rough-and-tumble world of electoral politics, our willful disbelief persisted despite the launch of venomous personal attacks on First Lady Hillary Clinton the day she accompanied her husband to the White House, the radicalization of the Republican Party in 1994 organized by Newt Gingrich, government shutdowns, and the ensuing impeachment of Bill Clinton in 1999 led by rogue prosecutor Kenneth Starr, who abandoned his fruitless investigation of political corruption to launch a persecutory inquest into Clinton's sexual life, provoking a constitutional crisis.[17]

This crisis was followed by a second one the next year, with the stolen presidential elections of 2000—political thuggery in full view of TV cameras. As the Florida vote recount proceeded and reports of physical assaults on poll workers by Republican operatives came in, the air became thick with the threat of political violence. You could cut the mounting climate of fear and dread with a knife, and Al Gore and old guard Democrats hesitated and relented, as if haunted and paralyzed by the unspoken traumatic memory of multiple political assassinations in the 1960s—from civil rights workers and John F. and Robert Kennedy to Medgar Evers, Martin Luther King, Malcolm X, and (later on) gay rights politician Harvey Milk. When the Republican partisans on the Supreme Court put a stop to the recount, Democratic politicians woke up to find themselves ejected from the political arena by a coup d'état and did not muster the courage to say so to the nation.

Meanwhile, Washington D.C. political insiders—what the French call *la classe politique*—told everyone to go back to work and get on with their lives. But of course what had happened was that George Bush, the twenty-first century's first "CEO- President"–elect, and his party had just fired the U.S. electorate as if they were so many redundant employees whose functions were now reassigned to the business sector, its media outlets, and well-funded political action committees. (The Supreme Court's *Citizens United* and *1965 Voting Rights Act* decisions legalizing unrestricted corporate political funding and gutting voter protections would later enshrine the theft in law once and for all.) Some refused to listen, and in January 2001 thousands of protestors turned out to greet George W. Bush's inauguration motorcade with rotten eggs and signs reading "Hail to the Thief!"[18]—an act of political defiance largely ignored by the major news organizations.

9/11, the Iraq Invasion, and the War on Terror

Not long afterwards, in the aftermath of 9/11 and during the buildup to the March 2003 invasion of Iraq, federal and local authorities, abetted by mainstream media such as the *New York Times,* unleashed a wave of intimidation and fearmongering against their own citizenry (invoking Saddam Hussein's fictional weapons of mass destruction and using Code Orange terrorist attack alerts based on outdated intelligence). Their actions ushered in what political philosopher Brian Massumi calls a new regime of counterfactuality and "felt reality of threat" as instruments of government. In other words, rule through fear and panic. In this kind of a state of emergency, threats require no verifiable referent, and "every possibility becomes a sure fact."[19]

9/11 effectively delivered into the hands of George Bush and the Republican Party a traumatized nation, and our new masters put citizens and residents through the political equivalent of collective military boot camp. Torn from the familiar surroundings of safety and home, we found ourselves stripped of our old identity; any allegiance to the old public virtues (respect for the Bill of Rights, the Geneva Conventions, and the rule of domestic and international law) was mocked and dismissed as quaint and soft by our new drill sergeants. From then on, a state of emergency replaced the rule of law and set itself up as the norm.[20] The U.S. launched a "war of choice" against Iraq that was also a massive experiment in extreme privatization and lawless power that extended to the armed services themselves: from the hiring of tens of thousands of private civilian contractors to handle military logistics and security in Iraq, to the practices of indefinite detention and torture of foreign nationals suspected of terrorism on flimsy evidence, to even the kidnapping and rendition of other foreign citizens by the CIA to unregulated "black sites" overseas for enhanced interrogation beyond the reach of the any legal system.

We were pressured to submit by leaders who claimed to protect us through politically expedient Code Orange terrorist attack warnings, and harassed and threatened us if we so much as voiced doubts concerning their new policies.[21] It would appear that the hope was to induce in the U.S. population "an infantile dread, an uncanny awe—and great expectations," an attitude of surrender followed by hoped-for transfiguration. Even military chiefs of staff and long-standing allies weren't spared: in the rush to invade Iraq, Donald Rumsfeld and his civilian deputies humiliated and removed reluctant generals who questioned the wisdom of going to war unprepared, while Colin Powell bullied hesitant allies as cowardly. As *Village Voice* writer Richard Goldstein, reprising the slang of gangsta rap, put it in his essay "Neo-Macho Man," Bush, Rumsfeld, and Powell were "the men," and the military and we civilians alike were their "bitches."[22]

Not to be outdone, politicians and media commentators welcomed the prospect of national renewal through war and called for strong interrogation tactics of those taken prisoner. Cable television series quickly followed suit. Fox Television's *24*, whose chief protagonist led a police anti-terrorist unit that employed torture and extrajudicial killings in each episode as regular tools of the trade, was the first in a line of shows to capitalize on the national crisis (Showtime's *Homeland* is the latest iteration). The Fox Television series was both a critical and popular success, and, according to investigative journalist Jane Meyer, the Pentagon in turn drew inspiration from the TV series for pursuing its techniques of torture, which always seemed to work on the small screen. Here, in cable and broadcast media, the process of identification with a lawless and cruel state was virtually complete, and I would argue we are still living with its political and legal consequences today as the War on Terror grinds on.[23]

Within the Beltway, the Bush Administration's rough tactics worked: intimidated congressional Democrats never countered with alternate themes and frames to those circulated by the White House and failed to muster effective congressional opposition to the war and the Patriot Act. [24] Amidst the drumbeat to war, many residents and citizens, less cowed than Democratic leaders, met the impending invasion with some of the largest anti-war demonstrations the nation had ever seen, but in the end there was no stopping the rush to invade and occupy Iraq.

As Russian-American journalist Masha Gessen has said, the destruction of the Twin Towers and its aftermath were the U.S. equivalent of Germany's Reichstag Fire in 1933, which paved the way for weakening the institutions of liberal democracy and the rule of law.[25] And it accelerated the process of hardening national political life already undertaken in earnest in the 1980s by an increasingly aggressive GOP as it pursued a take-no-prisoners approach to national and local politics that has helped create the violent political culture we are living in today.

George Bush's campaign manager Karl Rove was quick to capitalize on this emergent counterfactual regime by channeling Republican consultant Lee Atwater's highly effective attack ad campaigns of the 1980s. In 2002 and 2004 he launched overt media smears of decorated veterans such as Max Cleland (a triple amputee no less) and John Kerry (via the Swift Boating videos) whose sacrifices and actions Rove's henchmen belittled and mocked and whose patriotism they questioned. The Democratic candidates were slow to respond, later admitting they were simply unprepared for attacks on their military records.[26]

Unbeknownst to them, they had been forcibly thrust into the twilight zone of extreme political bullying in which no holds are barred and nothing is sacred. Not even military honor during a time of war, perhaps the last bastion of public respect in the U.S. Preemptive public attacks like these destabilize and intimidate opponents by making violently clear to one and all that their authors are supremely indifferent to any type of social, psychological or ethical boundary. The assailants strive to impress upon both actual and potential victims their literally *limitless* character, which exceeds all possible imaginings and logic.

What was Kerry's and Cleland's response? They contented themselves with countering with the "facts," in the apparent belief that facts could speak for themselves. In a word, they were victims of what linguist George Lakoff would term their own "communicational idealism," or the belief that language operates primarily and rationally at the level of concepts rather than through metaphor, repetition, and, last but not least, the neural networks of sensation and feeling that constitute the infrastructure of communication upon which successful verbal bullying depends.[27]

What they didn't realize is that extremely violent allegations endlessly repeated can succeed because they operate at the level of affect or emotion, creating confusion and anxiety among voters; and that by focusing solely on issues of character and intent that are difficult to refute, these attacks are able to bypass the accountability of factual discourse. They create an intimidating field of aggression that is unconstrained by fact-checking or empirical verification. [28]

Yet these smears should have not surprised them or us, for already during the 2000 presidential primaries, the Bush campaign targeted war hero and rival Republican John McCain by spreading a rumor suggesting that his adopted South Asian baby was a biracial love-child and that his Vietnam War experience of imprisonment and torture had unmanned him and rendered him mentally unstable. These attacks on McCain, Cleland, and Kerry left voters stunned, but with U.S. public opinion and media obsessed with questions of character, the virus of doubt spread quickly, infecting large numbers of mass viewers.

New York City as Laboratory of Intimidation and Fear

Outside the Beltway, Donald Trump's home turf of New York City also proved to be fertile ground for deepening the dark arts of political intimidation. It had already become the epicenter of the harsh new world of the financialized economy beginning in 1975 with New York City's fiscal crisis that allowed lending institutions to impose crippling austerity measures on the country's largest and most social-democratic municipality (eliminating free college tuition, affordable public transportation, etc.).

Then came the Volcker Recession (1980-82), which completed the city's subjection to the banking sector and Wall Street (and later, the unregulated derivatives markets of "shadow finance"). Pressures on companies by Wall Street to produce an unheard-of 20% return led to corporate takeovers, factory closings, massive layoffs, downsizing of middle management, and a surge in workplace bullying symbolized by the tyrannical or abusive boss much admired and promoted by the business press (see Chapter Two).

In this rougher environment, Republican Rudy Giuliani brought the bare-knuckled tactics he had been known for as U.S. Attorney for New York to the mayor's office during the 1990s (1993-2001). He refashioned and intensified the rough-and-tumble municipal politics, which had been dominated throughout much of the twentieth century by party machine patronage, back-room real estate deals, corrupt building-trades unions, and Mafia influence.

Still alive in this political culture were vivid memories of the Cold War smear used to bully and discredit political rivals, an art that was practiced without peer by New York attorney Roy Cohn, Senator Joe McCarthy's notorious former legal counsel and later Trump's lawyer and mentor. Courageous journalists like Bob Herbert and the late Wayne Barrett patiently chronicled how, through spectacular arrests of criminals and innocent civilians alike and the brutal removal of the homeless from the streets of New York, Giuliani installed a climate of intimidation and fear that targeted whites and the middle class as well as communities of color and the poor.[29]

Perfecting the use of punitive threats and retaliation, Giuliani cowed dissident city administrators into silence through smearing the reputations of his critics and sending the police to rough up citizens. He even went so far as to declare all city dwellers to be so many "law-breakers in waiting," thereby edging a climate of fear towards one of terror: no one, high or low, was safe from the long arm of the mayor and the NYPD.[30] Eventually, even New Yorkers, whose developed instinct for pushing back in a rough environment they like to see reflected in the aggressiveness of city politicians, seemed to grow weary of Giuliani's thuggish behavior during his second term. However, his stirring press conference amidst the ruins of the Twin Towers on September 11th imparted a new sheen to Giuliani's tarnished reputation (Oprah Winfrey hailed him as "America's mayor"), and the terrorist attacks vastly expanded opportunities for political intimidation that his Republican successor Michael Bloomberg (2002-14) ably exploited for political advantage.[31]

This long political history continues up through the Obama Administration, but to understand its persistent power in contemporary politics in the next chapter we will look at the wider culture, focusing on the workplace and the media. There, a revolution was taking place in the limits of acceptable public speech and behavior that enabled right-wing agendas and the candidacy of Donald Trump. My fundamental point will be that the different arenas of the workplace, media, and politics operated as so many different locations of aggression that worked together to create a general public culture of intimidation. The example and achieved legitimacy of behaviors in one arena (say the media or workplace) can have the effect of authorizing analogous conduct in other domains of civil society (for example, politics) and vice versa. Their synergy thereby produced a reciprocal legitimation of like practices and actions of the harshest kind.

CHAPTER TWO

Intimidation and Bullying in the Wider Culture: The Workplace and the Media

> If we are to confront Fear, American Style, it is here, in the workplace, that we must begin and end, for it is in the workplace that men and women in the contemporary United States most consistently encounter personal coercion and repressive fear. Though heavy, the personal toll of workplace fear is not the only cause of concern: its political repercussions are equally, if not more, consequential.
>
> Corey Robin, *Fear: The History of a Political Idea*

> A deadly combination of economic rationalism, increasing competition, "downsizing," and the current fashion for tough, dynamic, "macho," management styles, have created a culture in which bullying can thrive, producing "toxic" workplaces.
>
> "Workplace Bullying: The Silent Epidemic," Editorial, *British Medical Journal.*[32]

Part and parcel of the deeper history of practices of public humiliation and political intimidation are changes happening in the wider culture in the 1980s and 1990s that fostered a coarser public climate and legitimized violent verbal and non-verbal behavior in daily life.

Harsh Climate

We think we know who they are: They cut you off on the highway, they taunt you to your face, mock you behind your back, smirk at you from the TV screen, standing always beyond reach. They are everywhere and anywhere, from the schoolyard to the boardroom, the office cubicle to your local bar. They come unbidden, visiting violence upon the unsuspecting and the fearful alike. They now lurk even in your pocket wherever you go, and you can feel the buzz as trolls spew 140-character poison to anyone and everyone. Even at home you can't get away from the pervasive climate of intimidation and disrespect: you turn on your TV or laptop and there they are, injecting venom and fear through old and new media.

Requiring little or no provocation, they are poised to strike at the first sign of weakness—or courage. For they tolerate no one, no one but their own kind—belligerent aggressors ready to declare who's fit to speak, to listen, and to submit. As Trump said to then Fox News host Megyn Kelly in a subsequent interview after publicly demeaning her after the first Republican debate, "But you gotta get over it. Fight back, do what you have to do."

The violence, the intimidation: you think you're ready—perhaps you've experienced it before—but still when it happens, especially to you, your person, your body, the body politic, its sheer power, speed, and intensity bypass whatever defenses you have. From the edges of consciousness, the aggressors rush up, attacking and screaming in your face, "You're nothing but" scum, a liberal, a feminist, a Muslim, a self-hating Jew, an immigrant, a Bernie Bro, a Putin stooge, a "nasty woman," a faggot, a loser. Bewildered, we're thrown off balance—we can't believe it is happening.

Be it again or for the first time, it seems to make no difference. The hormonal response wells up—"fight or flight"—but it's already too late; something has slipped under our skin and taken over. Disoriented and at a loss for words, we have the creeping realization that whatever our sense of self was *before*, we can never quite retrieve it again. Thanks to bullying we find ourselves forced into a life divided between what we are—or rather, what we have become—and a former sovereign self that the bullies have persuaded us we've lost. Something or someone has intruded—and violently so— and changed us. Our self-representation has been wrested away, and we are, as it were, beyond our own reach. Something else is there, intimately there, a power—and a weakness—that we can't control.[33] Captive of our potential weakness and the aggressors' potential violence, we have entered into the infinite, fearful regress and fact of future threat.[34] If there wasn't a relationship before, there is one now, unbreakable even as it breaks us.

If our sense of humiliation is severe enough, we respond by reasserting ourselves through bullying others in turn, or in the case of the extreme distress of isolated young U.S. males consumed with self-loathing, taking a gun and shooting down teachers and students in classrooms and hallways before dispatching their abject selves to oblivion.[35] With bullying the unthinkable has happened, and we feel *betrayed* by both the aggressors and ourselves—*"How did they dare?" "How did I let it happen?"*—and there begins the endless search for a response. So perhaps in a society still in thrall to the gospel of the free market, let us turn to the private sector and its media outlets for some answers.

Ground Zero: Financial and Managerial Revolution in the Workplace

The year is 1980. It was the end of the Carter Administration, and a wave of hyperinflation was convulsing the economy, prompting Paul Volcker of the Federal Reserve to brutally increase the prime lending rate banks charge to customers to 21.5%. The effects were immediate and profound. In a single stroke, the mortgage market collapsed, student lending vanished, loans dried up to companies struggling to meet daily operations costs such as payroll, sending thousands of them into bankruptcy.

Inflation subsided, but the unemployment rate rose to nearly 11%. In addition, one third of existing savings and loans associations worth at least $400 billion failed, having overextended themselves with long-term loans to clients at rates well below the new rate at which these banks themselves could borrow new money, costing taxpayers over $132 billion. [36] The great Volcker Recession (1980-82) was underway. Meanwhile, commercial banks began to offer well-to-do clients certificates of deposit (CDs) that earned more than the inflation rate of 14%, for a minimum deposit of $10,000. Finance capital got a taste of something new: returns on fixed-income investments not seen since the 1920s.

The financialization of the U.S. economy had begun. Firms discovered that they could make higher short-term returns through speculative financial investments using borrowed money (such as highly leveraged corporate mergers and exotic financial instruments and derivatives like mortgage-backed securities) than through the traditional means of direct investment in fixed capital formation (that is, machines, buildings, etc.) and training workers in order to increase productivity and output.

This made an already bad situation worse, for management by the mid-1970s had decoupled workers' wages from productivity gains. And even later when the introduction of digital technologies began to produce substantial increases in productivity in U.S. firms, workers saw no benefit. The stagnation of U.S. household wages had begun, and it continues today. [37]

When in 1999 the Republican Congress and the Clinton White House repealed the Glass-Steagall Act of 1933 and lifted barriers to banks speculating with customers' federally guaranteed bank deposits, they gave a tremendous boost to finance industry mergers and consolidations and fueled unchecked growth in shadow finance's derivative markets. In evaluating companies' financial health, optimistic expectations of rising asset prices replaced prospective cash flows. [38] The financial sector's exponential growth was also fueled by rising consumer debt in the form of mortgages.

(Today one would have to also add student debt.) By the 2000s, in the U.S. the finance industry generated 41% of all corporate profits, compared to 16% between 1973 and 1985, and constituted up to 31% of New York City's tax base.[39]

With each passing year, servicing the costs of those debt-financed non-productive investments—stocks, bonds, real estate, and mergers—together with the new exorbitant executive salaries would take a bigger bite out of operating budgets, leaving less and less for capital improvements, employee training, and workers' wages. In this brave new world, there was even less room for applying expansive Keynesian-inspired government economic measures, which favor growth and consumer demand in times of economic contraction, and in their stead the doctrine of fiscal austerity and corporate tax cuts became ascendant. The way was paved for the radical redistribution in wealth and income that led to the historically high disparities we know today.

As cash poured in from overseas to take advantage of interest rates offered by U.S. banks, the dollar rocketed to new highs against foreign currencies in the years that followed. Investors began converting their equities to CDs, and powerful shareholders (mutual funds) and Wall Street, desperate to maintain stock prices, responded by putting pressure on company management to equal the performance. The 20% corporate return was born and with it the go-go 1980s of a resurgent financial sector, junk (high-yield) bonds, corporate raiders, leveraged buyouts (LBOs), and merger mania.

But it also entailed the selling off of newly acquired companies' profitable divisions, factory closings, wage "give-backs" to management, massive layoffs of workers, and the downsizing of middle management to pay off leveraged debt in a climate of relentless international competition driven by a strong dollar and by Japanese steel and automobile industries. And with it came ruthless short-term management and a new creature, the bullying boss.[40]

This latest avatar in CEO personae, he—not she—was announced with great fanfare on April 21, 1980 in *Fortune*

Magazine's cover story, "America's Toughest Bosses," which listed the top ten heads of corporations who qualified. Half-critical, half-admiring, the article started a tradition of surveys repeated in the 1980s and 1990s in *Fortune*'s pages every four or five years. They chronicled the ascendancy of this new American corporate figure, which radicalized the older militarized corporate management model of autocratic command and control inherited from the Second World War.[41] The older model was embodied by the cool, rational Cold War bureaucratic style of Robert McNamara, CEO of Ford Motor Co. and later Secretary of Defense under Presidents Kennedy and Johnson.

During the self-doubting 1970s, it was briefly discredited in the business world by Theory Y Management techniques and sensitivity training, and no sooner were they gone than the older model returned in the form of the aloof yet mercurial CEO, manipulative, abusive, arbitrary, and vindictive, and, to the delight of the press, often colorful and quirky. The original *Fortune* article quoted one chief executive's management philosophy thus: "Leadership is demonstrated when the ability to inflict pain is confirmed." A later survey would characterize these men as "outstanding taskmasters" who were "demanding and hard to please" and with a "penchant for psychological oppression" in whose presence an atmosphere of fear abounds. [42]

The Bullying Boss

By the early 1990s the U.S. business press had christened this new figure the "bullying boss" and followed with admiring nicknames such as "Chainsaw." Employees and executive staff added a few of their own: "Loose Cannon," "Old Blood and Guts," "Rambo in Pinstripes," "Jack the Ripper," and "Prince of Darkness."[43] (Less impressed by this male personality type, female workers offered one of their own: "BSD," or "Big Swinging Dick.") Endowed with the outsized attributes of rogue soldiers, freewheeling entrepreneurs, or bad-boy celebrities, rather than those of rational managers of large bureaucratic enterprises, a new American folk hero was born who was afforded every indulgence and every reprieve.

The earliest names included Donald Rumsfeld (CEO of G.D. Searle Pharmaceuticals), Steve Jobs (NEXT Computing), Andrew Grove (Intel), Jack Welch (General Electric), Carl Icahn (TWA), and Harvey and Bob Weinstein (Miramax Films). Thirty years later many of these names are still with us—and so is their management style. As business columnist and gadfly Stanley Bing wrote in the early 1990s:

> So it is today, where bullying behavior is encouraged and rewarded in a range of business enterprises. The style itself is applauded in boardrooms and in-house organs like *Business Week* as "tough," "no nonsense," "hard as nails." When you see these code words, you know you're dealing with the bully boss... [T]hanks to the admiration in which bully management is held in the American business establishment, the fledgling who studies under the heads of the successful bully masters the techniques and becomes one, too.[44]

In the business press and workplace, stories and anecdotes of public humiliations and even physical fear proliferated, as if the mythically high-handed, intimidating methods of the noisy factory floor had been transferred to the quieter cubicles and offices of middle and upper management, where twelve- to fourteen-hour days in some companies became the norm. Even private life wasn't safe from the depredations of bosses: one CEO reportedly called a senior manager thirty-one times over one Thanksgiving weekend; another chief executive insisted on speaking to a female manager for twenty minutes as she underwent labor; and the owner/manager of a large family business physically threatened his wife and daughter before terminating them.[45] The introduction of performance-related pay and the promise of stock options in the 1980s and 1990s intensified still further the focus on the bottom line and helped recruit upper management to the task of downsizing their less senior colleagues by whetting their greed and buying executives' tolerance of CEOs' abusive methods.[46]

Consequently, office workers with little job security found themselves squeezed between the drive for short-term profits and the much vaunted "discipline of the marketplace" that presumably rewarded success and punished failure. They also found themselves caught in the jarring contradiction between, on the one hand, Human Resources departments' new rhetoric of "teamwork" and "flexibility" that promised informal, cooperative relationships, promoted the value of interpersonal skills, and incited employees to ever greater personal investment in their jobs, and, on the other, the day-to-day experience of bullying that either reinforced hierarchies of authority and status (teams working under an authoritarian leader) or sought to introduce them in settings where they were not visibly acknowledged. It was a system of one-way loyalty that empowered senior managers as rarely before.[47]

In the U.S. the public theater of firing employees quickly became a well-rehearsed one in offices, especially as security concerns mounted with the spread of computers to all employees: after receiving the pink slip, like so many criminals under arrest by the police, hapless workers are relieved of their company IDs, their passwords are cancelled, and then they are escorted to their desks, where, under the watchful eye of armed security guards, they are ordered to clear out their personal effects before being marched out of the building in front of astonished coworkers. Firing became even the stuff of TV melodrama, as in the reality TV show *The Apprentice* (2004-) coproduced and hosted by real estate mogul Donald Trump, who played the role of a boss much feared and admired by his young interviewees, who compete to be retained by him to help run one of his companies. The climax of every narrative cycle was sealed by the CEO informing an unhappy contestant, "You're fired!" It is a sadistic spectacle of dominance and humiliation whose pleasures disavow what many viewers fear most in their own lives.

Short-Term Greed, Long-Term Insecurity

By the 1990s a system of "short-term greed and long-term insecurity" was well in place, and it represented the latest avatar in the corporate workplace of what U.S. sociologist C. Wright Mills termed long ago "the American system of organized irresponsibility."[48] There were even companies that regularly fired 10–15 percent of their workforce every nine to twelve months in order to create the climate of uncertainty and fear deemed by management to be effective in enforcing employee submissiveness and discipline. It was the violent extension of a management method of constant evaluation invented by Jack Welch, Jr., the very aggressive former CEO of General Electric, under the name of "forced ranking," of workers' performance related to shifting metrics of "excellence" and productivity.[49]

As a result, accusations of poor work performance became a smokescreen for deflecting employees' response to unacceptable behaviors and to the unfair firing of coworkers. In a climate of fear, for executives short on ideas about how to run their businesses, intimidation and bullying had the advantage of passing as an effective management method. The pressures—and excuses—for bullying in the workplace were perhaps even worse in the public sector as Republican and Democratic politicians slashed budgets for public services and imposed "marketplace philosophies in an under-resourced" environment.[50] Even the U.S. Post Office became a "profit center of excellence" meant to compete with private sector enterprises; it also became a center of workplace violence and shootings.[51]

How did Human Resources departments respond? All too often, faced with evidence of abusive acts by a domineering boss, they—then as now—tended to interpret them as "clashes of personalities," in which institutional and economic factors tended to vanish in favor of purely personal and psychological ones. This is replicated by the grievance system—if one exists at all in the workplace—that reduces everything to the level of "individual complaint." In such an environment targets of intimidation and abuse are often perceived to be the problem and are pursued again—this time as scapegoats whose removal is deemed by Human Resources departments to be the most expedient response by management.[52]

To this day, little has been said in the U.S. media or public discussion about how the continuing obsession with short-term profits and the awarding of exorbitant executive pay laid the foundation for a surge in abusive behavior in the workplace. Even less has been said about how the introduction of "best-practices" of flexible employment, outsourcing of traditional company tasks, and the reclassification of workers as "independent contractors" have opened the door to "management by terror"[53] in workplaces already left to the tender mercies of "at-will employment." A workplace regime dating from the nineteenth century and unique to the U.S., "at-will employment" means that employees never know from one day to the next who could lose their livelihood—and with it access to medical insurance.[54] It was an infernal circle: according to labor economist David Gordon in *Fat and Mean*, in the 1980s as employees' wages were cut and workers' incentives evaporated, aggressive supervision of a demoralized workforce by the overworked remaining middle managers increased exponentially.[55]

Thus this harsh workplace environment—where most working adults spend the majority of their waking hours—constituted a rough civic education in the undemocratic ways of power and authority. It was also one that was reinforced and legitimated by a revolution in the limits of acceptable public speech and behavior in the media.

The Media Sphere

Outside the workplace, a new culture of intimidation began to emerge in U.S. mass culture. Already in the 1970s macho populism arose in the figures of Clint Eastwood, Charles Bronson, Sylvester Stallone, and Chuck Norris (and followed by Michael Douglas in the 1980s), creatures of male injury and resentment, who in action and sexual avenger films reclaimed American male honor and prerogative lost in the aftermath of the civil rights, women's, and gay and lesbian movements, the defeat in Vietnam, and early globalization's massive deindustrialization of the U.S. economy. [56] This marked the beginning of the appropriation and exploitation of an aggrieved (white) masculinity by the media and politicians.

Integral to this process was the contrasting cultural figure of the intimidating angry black male, whom, as writer Ishmael Reed reminds us, mainstream entertainment and news converted from a political cliché and blaxploitation film hero to a straightforward symbol of sociopathology (mugger, rapist, pimp, drug dealer, gang member) His naturally violent and shiftless character both victimized whites and justified the dominant culture's extremely aggressive treatment of black men. He became a cover for the violent expression of white rage. [57]

The examples are countless, starting with the Bernard Goetz New York subway shootings (1984) and the Republican Willie Horton presidential ad campaign (1988) to the widely reported cases of the Boston murderer Charles Stuart, who blamed a black man for killing his pregnant wife (1989) and the Central Park Jogger, who was the presumed victim of "wilding" black youth (1989). This last case prompted the entry of Trump into politics for the first time. [58] Other examples include the beating of Rodney King by the LAPD and subsequent riots and trial (1991-92) and the sensationalized coverage of the O.J. Simpson trial (1994-95).

According to legal scholar Michelle Alexander, even more crucial to these developments were the War on Drugs, "three strikes" laws, and massive incarceration of young African-American men, which by 2000 had resulted in, for example, 55% of the adult black male population of Chicago being classed as felons or former felons. [59] The media's and law enforcement's obsessive profiling of black men as criminally violent had deadly consequences in the form of unprovoked police shootings that to this day are invariably excused by the prosecutors, judges, and juries who accept police officers' claims that they killed out of fear for their lives. The video recordings of these incidents that regularly surfaced in 2016 and 2017 and roiled U.S. elections stand as the continuation of the older spectacle of repressive violence visited upon the African-American community in preceding decades.

At the same time a new tone and style of public discourse broke through over the airwaves. Part and parcel of the exploding culture wars[60] and exploiting the fracturing of national media audiences afforded by the rise of cable TV, AM radio and TV talk shows arose, hosted by Don Imus (1971-2007), Howard Stern (1982-) and Morton Downey, Jr. (1986-92) and later Rush Limbaugh (1988-), Bill O'Reilly (1996-2017), Bill Maher (*Politically Incorrect*, 1993-2002), and Glenn Beck (2006-). They revolutionized acceptable public speech by provoking and channeling audiences' pent-up (male) rage against, alternately, people of color, liberals, feminists, leftists, queers, welfare recipients, and immigrants, smashing the last remnants of respectful speech of the old broadcast media. The mainstreaming of public expressions of hate was well underway.

A new televised male spectacle emerged in political talk shows such as *Capitol Gang* (1988-2005) and the *McLaughlin Group* (1982-2016), followed later by Chris Matthews's *Hardball* (1994-) and *Hannity and Colmes* (1996-2009), and featuring political personalities such as Newt Gingrich (former Republican Speaker of the House), James Carville (former advisor to Bill Clinton), Pat Buchanan (former aide to Richard Nixon), and David Horowitz (ex-leftist neoconservative).[61] Speaking over and shouting down liberal or progressive guests were commonplace in talk shows, and even physical assault, in the case of Downey and O'Reilly, were not to be ruled out.[62]

Public fascination with media spectacles of dominance drove up ratings and aggressive politicians were quick to exploit it.

Reality TV and Social Media

Perhaps even more insidious were the reality TV shows, beginning with the American version of *Survivor* (1997-) and later on, *The Apprentice* (2004-) and *American Idol* (2002-) that staged extreme competition between participants and cruel theaters of humiliation in various settings from exotic locales in the wild to executive suites and talent shows. Appealing to very American dreams of material gain and success among contestants and viewers alike, they were a potent spectacle in a national mass culture that promotes promises of individual success, self-transformation, and fulfillment, even fame and glamour, through individual entrepreneurship, relentless aggression, and luck: the greater the promise, the greater the personal desire and vulnerability—and the greater the likelihood of public humiliation.[63]

Talk shows' and reality TV's revolution in acceptable public speech arguably laid the groundwork for the cyberbullying that would explode with the rise of social media twenty years later. Already the advent in the 1990s of new Internet-based communication technologies—like email, anonymous listservs, websites, AOL's Instant Messenger (AIM), and blogs—created a new digital sociality that increased exponentially the opportunities for verbal and psychological abuse, and by virtue of their speed, ubiquity, and ease of use, they quickly became the means of choice for intimidating others. In the late 2000s, by shifting and blurring the already fluid boundaries between private and public speech, and between private and public networks, social media—like MySpace, Facebook, Twitter, and later Instagram—vastly increased avenues of direct personal and group communication, self-publicity, and self-promotion, but also by the same token they increased the means of public intimidation, defamation, slander, rumormongering, and stalking.

A wave of U.S. suicide cases attributed to cyberbullying was not long in coming, including most spectacularly that of Tyler Clementi, a gay first-year student at Rutgers University in New Jersey, whose tryst his roommate video-recorded and then posted on Twitter.[64] Much is heard in the media about teenage cyberbullying, primarily because public discussions of bullying and psychological intimidation have traditionally focused on the schoolyard or cafeteria as sites of abuse, but also because adolescents were the earliest and most passionate users of social media. However, adults were quick to follow suit in all spheres of life.

Unfortunately, in the U.S. legal tradition there are few safeguards against extremely aggressive practices of public intimidation and denigration in most areas of national life. To begin with, there is the powerful legacy of civil rights protections going back to Title VII of the 1964 Civil Rights Act that target only discriminatory acts against classes of persons. These protections regard primarily the spheres of the workplace and commercial and public services, not political life or the media. Thus, in the U.S., sexual harassment in the workplace falls under the logic of legislation banning discrimination but that is not the case for intimidation or bullying, which are not covered by existing law unless the victim is targeted in terms of his or her belonging to a protected group (race, color, religion, sex, national origin, disability, age, or marital status).[65]

Then there is the "absolutist" doctrine of freedom of expression as interpreted by U.S. courts over the last ninety years: all speech, however hateful and injurious it may be, is protected by law unless it leads immediately to acts of *physical* violence. In this tradition freedom of speech is not balanced with other values such as privacy, dignity, safety, equality, respect, and so forth. As a result, all attempts in the 1980s and 1990s to establish hate speech codes regulating racist utterances (commonly found in Europe) came to grief in U.S. courts.[66]

In our coarsening public life it was perhaps only a matter of time before an abusive boss and media celebrity would take the national stage.

CHAPTER THREE

Enter Trump: The Tyrannical CEO and White Entrepreneur as Capitalist Folk Hero

> I don't do it for the money. I've got enough, much more than I'll ever need. I do it to do it. Deals are my art form... I like making deals, preferably big deals. That's how I get my kicks.
>
> Donald Trump with Tony Schwartz, *Trump: The Art of the Deal*

> Moderation is a fatal thing. Nothing succeeds like excess.
>
> Oscar Wilde

> Now, today, this kind of hateful language and name-calling is happening again; only this time it's occurring in the fungible confines of these yet-to-be United States of America. I say *again* because it has happened before with the genocide and removal of Native American Indians; with African-Americans during slavery and Reconstruction; with Asians during the territorial expansion westward and the internment camps during World War II in the 1940s.
>
> Quincy Troupe, "My Take" 67

The Question

What will we be after Election Day? Discarded employees or disenfranchised voters? Such was the question nagging anxious voters, summer and fall of 2016. On November 8th, CEO and Republican nominee Donald Trump provided the answer: both.

One fallout of the release in October 2016 of the tape of

Trump bragging about sexually assaulting women was to redirect debate back to the workplace, from which Trump first came, and its abusive power relations. After all, the workplace is where "Rambos in Pinstripes" and "Big Swinging Dicks" still thrive today and where gropers enjoy the greatest immunity. Yet except for a passing nod to his TV franchise *The Apprentice*, even at this late stage of the election, pundits and editors paid little or no attention to the extent to which Donald Trump's tactics of intimidation first achieved public legitimacy by virtue of changes in U.S. corporate management and media culture in the 1980s, and how Trump parlayed them into a potent political campaign.

By late October, Trump had smashed all remaining boundaries of acceptable political discourse in an already harsh political climate, and then—as now—commentators never stopped focusing obsessively on his dysfunctional personality. What they forgot was that while Trump may be a violent narcissist, not all narcissists can become Trump, capitalist folk hero and Republican presidential nominee.[68] And if Trump the politician represents the unvarnished expression of the Republicans' decades-long "Southern strategy" of stoking white voters' fears in the face of economic uncertainty and shifting demographics, the white nationalist content of his campaign and now new administration is amplified by not only a compliant media but also his mesmerizing entrepreneurial style that respects no social or ethical limits as its relentlessly seeks political advantage and opportunities against all comers.

Trump's powerful combining of racist and misogynistic content with his freewheeling entrepreneurialism formed the basis of much of his broad appeal, which took the Republican and Democratic establishments and U.S. commentariat by surprise. [69] But it shouldn't have. Few businessmen or politicians were as poised as Trump was to take full advantage of the coarseness of public life in the throes of globalization, with its hardened workplace culture and media sphere that tolerated or even encouraged the most aggressive behavior and speech. His campaign was a breakthrough that unleashed frightening and uncontrollable public dynamics, and the overtly violent political culture and white nationalism that he has mainstreamed risks shaping U.S. elections for years to come.

Trump the Entrepreneur

In all respects Trump's successful strategy to become the nominee of the Republican Party was a textbook hostile takeover bid of a corporation—memorably dramatized by Michael Douglas as corporate raider Gordon Gekko in Oliver Stone's 1987 film *Wall Street*—that appealed to the shareholders (the party base) to revolt against a smug and inept management (the Republican establishment) by promising a price that could not be beat: unalloyed expression of their voter outrage at the status quo in a bid "to make [white] America great again."

Trump is a proud graduate of the Wharton School of Business, which in the late twentieth century spawned some of the most destructive businessmen and Wall Street operators (associated with Lewis Ranieri's notorious Salomon Brothers gang) who created mortgage-backed securities (bonds), those weapons of mass destruction of "shadow finance."[70] Yet he is also an independent businessman—real estate mogul—who affects none of the smooth talk of corporate communications but all the rough street speech of undersocialized Wall Street bond traders and the outsized personality of freewheeling entrepreneurs, for whom every day is a new day and what you lose today you can win back tomorrow. Each day represents an opportunity, each day a new move in which anything is negotiable. Action and movement are everything; he radiates the pure macho energy of risk and success: if you stand still, you die.

The original tabloid businessman turned politician, whose tumultuous business dealings (3,500 lawsuits) and private life (two divorces, countless girlfriends) fill the scandal sheets, Trump is the pure entrepreneurial subject that still fascinates large segments of the public in our new Gilded Age. This is what billionaire financial data and media CEO and former

Republican mayor of New York Michael Bloomberg failed to understand when he denounced Trump at the Democratic 2016 convention as a poor businessman.

Successful management of accumulated wealth or a corporation is not what excites Trump. Like most entrepreneurs, as opposed to senior executives, overseeing the day-to-day operations of a company and meeting quarterly expectations of investors are not particularly what attracts him or even what he would be good at. What interests Trump is as much the excitement of the hunt as the result, high-stakes gambling as much as the bottom line, the glitz and worth of his "brand" as much as his net wealth.[71] He said as much in the opening lines cited above of his 1987 bestseller, *Trump: The Art of the Deal*, for those who had eyes to see past the braggadocio. It was published at the height of the first stock market bubble of the financialized economy pumped up by corporate junk bonds, leveraged buyouts (LBOs), and the first wave of mortgage-backed securities.

As owner and CEO of a large family business, Trump enjoys the clout of a chief executive without any accountability to a board of directors or aggressive mutual fund managers. Unlike George W. Bush, touted by Republicans back in 2000 as the first "CEO President," he comes across as his own man and beholden to no one (clan, party, or donors). He possesses the magical freedom and irresponsibility of celebrities while embodying the savvy worldliness of the makers and shakers of capitalist America.

Trump made this more than clear at the outset in the first televised Republican debate, hosted by Fox News in Cleveland in August 2015. In response to the panel's first question, posed by Brett Baier, which asked the ten assembled candidates who would *not* support the winner of the Republican nomination, Trump stood alone with his hand raised and even refused to pledge that he wouldn't run as an independent candidate. Given his wealth and widespread name recognition, it was a credible threat of a nature rarely seen in national political life. The public bullying of an entire political party before a national cable TV audience by one of its own candidates was unprecedented and broke with the Republicans' ethos of loyalty and discipline to which even earlier insurgent populist candidate Pat Buchanan submitted in the 1990s.

Trump embodied a new American folk hero, the bullying boss, who was afforded every indulgence and every reprieve. As we saw in Chapter Two, like many of the earliest names promoted thirty years ago by an admiring business press—Donald Rumsfeld, Andrew Grove, Jack Welch, Carl Icahn, and Harvey and Bob Weinstein—he is very much with us. But unlike most of them, he was born to wealth, became a media celebrity in his own right, and was a political outsider who now rules the land.

Trump's brilliant coup was to make the new over-the-top management ethos part of his brand and to convert the well-rehearsed humiliating theater of firing employees familiar to office workers into the stuff of TV melodrama. Thanks to *The Apprentice*, he quickly secured his status as global household word and embodiment of the new abusive management style. The way had been cleared to translate his successful brand into enormous political capital that he then cashed in.

Trump's Negative Identity Politics: From Cold War Smearing to Entrepreneurial Bullying

Bad behavior is nothing new, but what is singular in the current reign of the public bully is the interplay of economic and non-economic humiliations and indignities encountered in daily life under globalized market economies and the endless War on Terror. Arguably, this is what lends contemporary bullying and intimidation its widespread reach and edge, from the school and the workplace to the media and political spheres to cyberspace. This is the culture in which Donald Trump can thrive. If today the workplace and the media rival the school as vehicles for educating people in the ways of power and forms of citizenship, then CEO Trump was uniquely poised to capitalize on this new political culture of intimidation and fear.

By virtue of his outsized persona, he has been successful in articulating a sense of personal grievance as a collective one. Yet most (white) mainstream and non-mainstream journalists and commentators did not see him coming and missed one of the most consequential political stories of our era. Among the exceptional few were filmmaker Michael Moore, who issued desperate warnings to the Democratic establishment during the primaries; the dean of modern U.S. conservatism William F. Buckley, founder of the *National Review,* who in 2000 already viewed him as a credible candidate worth recruiting to the Republican Party; and, further back, GOP consultant Samuel Francis, who foresaw the emergence of a candidate like Trump representing middle-class populism, who would achieve what nationalist candidate Pat Buchanan failed to do.[72]

Writers living in New York or working for New York–based publications, like the *New Yorker*'s Adam Gopnik, were caught unawares and fell into a panic once his primary campaign met with success. Other, more seasoned political observers like the *New York Times*'s Paul Krugman dismissed Trump out of hand, perhaps because he was *too* familiar a figure in the local media and society pages and roundly disliked by all.[73] They couldn't imagine Trump, a local boy if there ever was one, from the outer boroughs of Brooklyn and Queens, translating his rough business practices and crass personality into a successful political career, much less one he could take beyond the city limits to the national stage.[74]

Even newer Brooklyn-based publications like *Jacobin* and *n+1*, professing to expound leftist analysis of the economy, politics, and culture, discounted his candidacy as merely idiosyncratic or self-destructive. They couldn't imagine him as a potential political force to be reckoned with—embodying as Trump does the most distasteful and vulgar aspects of mass culture thriving in today's free-market society. Familiarity may breed contempt, but in this case it also bred a political blindness betraying an underlying cultural elitism that they shared with more mainstream writers like Gopnik and Krugman. Only former *New York Times* theater critic and oped columnist Frank Rich, with his deep knowledge of popular culture, saw early on beyond Trump's crass personality and appreciated the disruptive threat Trump's raw style and rough populism posed to the political and media establishments. Nonetheless, he, too, expressed doubts that Trump's candidacy would succeed.[75]

We ignore the profoundly compelling psychological and social dimensions of contemporary capitalist culture at our peril. The Russian-American journalist Masha Gessen has argued that what is missing in U.S. public culture is a shared narrative that mobilizes people's hopes of a better collective future. I couldn't agree more. In the U.S. there already exists a powerful discourse that fills that role, but it is one that sustains the violent politics of Trump and his Republican allies: that individual initiative, aggressive entrepreneurship, and free markets unimpeded by government interference are the royal road to personal fulfillment and social betterment. It functions in the wider culture virtually as an American birthright.

For many, it is woven into the very fabric of the American Dream and undergirds a fierce sense of entitlement shared by ordinary people and CEOs alike. This potent capitalist culture is the basis of that peculiar strand of American populism that is at once violently anti-elitist and stands in awe of successful, self-made men and women, especially from the business world, and the world of wealth they populate.[76]

*

*   *

Bullying and intimidation have become a special form of power widespread today. It is more than just exerting pressure; it is far more consequential. It connects subjective, individual experiences with those of society itself. Targets of repeated attacks can lose not only control over their self-representation but even their capacity to pursue their studies or training, work productively, enjoy effective voice in public discourse, or run for office.

Trump is perfectly aware of this. Educated in the Cold War art of the political smear by his mentor and lawyer Roy Cohn (Senator Joe McCarthy's notorious former legal counsel), Trump expertly engages in stigmatizing the identity of opponents. Had we thought that the stake had been driven into the heart of the Cold War culture of fear and intimidation once and for all, the War on Terror should already have disabused us of that illusion. But overlooked by pundits and reporters is the peculiarly entrepreneurial twist Trump lends to the older bullying enterprise: he introduces an aggressive timeline in which the future is everything and the present and past exist only to be overcome. Trump successfully melds, as perhaps no other before him, the entrepreneur's and the politician's shared obsession with the short term, in which the future is pure promise of change and transformation of which he, Trump, is the sole broker. This is the sales pitch of most every successful U.S. politician, businessman, and confidence man.[77]

Trump stands between our "fear of the future and hope for success." His brokering of the future is a particularly powerful proposition in our volatile post-2008 economic context where accumulated grievances and uncertainty rule. As political philosopher Brian Massumi has put it, "Capitalism, always a far-from-equilibrium system, is becoming ever more so. *The same multiplier mechanism that promises future satisfaction makes it exponentially less certain.*"[78] Instability is at once the engine of possibility and hope and the fomenter of dread and fear.

Let me explain Trump's entrepreneurial style of character assassination. It is twofold. First, and more recognizably, allegations about an opponent's character or motives are by nature difficult to disprove, as in the question "When did you stop beating your wife?" Second, and perhaps more originally, Trump's accusations present the advantage of imprisoning the victim in a mocked identity whereby she—or he—has no future, only a discredited past and present. So a *loser* is not someone who has lost an election or a deal; rather, it is someone who *always* loses and is a perpetual victim of circumstance.

Trump on the other hand, *he* speaks as a free man from the future: in truth, ever ready for the latest deal, he has no identity, only a future-oriented readiness to negotiate anything (real estate, the Constitution, the rule of law) and with anyone (Putin, Kim Jong-un, etc.). Others have an identity, which he names and denigrates as entirely deficient, disabling, and limited. Such is Trump's negative identity politics that seeks to caricature and dishonor opponents' personhood.

The Defiant White Man: The Method is the Message

The real identity he embodies needs no naming: the great free-born white American male. His violence signifies liberty and authenticity. Part of his peculiar power and privilege as inveterate aggressor is his ability to fend off attacks through his openly acknowledged self-interest and penchant for violence, pre-emptive self-parody (his campy hair, his orange complexion), and even claims of victimhood (at the hands of women, immigrants, liberals, Muslims, protestors, the press, the judiciary, etc.).

In Trump aggression and a very traditional conservative sense of grievance against an overwhelming modernity are intimately intertwined. One's own weakness or vulnerability is the fault of maligned others. It is an aggressive discourse that is all controlling but never accountable, a form of victimhood that, according to historian Robert O. Paxton in his essay "The Five Stages of Fascism," is endemic to authoritarian and fascist movements.[79] It promises the reassertion of violent personal and collective sovereignty over feared others through identification with a charismatic and sadistic leader.[80] In free-market economies like the U.S., this most likely means a businessman.

So what may seem hysterical or out of control is also a method. And one that often worked through the presidential campaign and first months in office. Trump adds to the Republican record of electoral skullduggery and intimidation an inescapable psychological and affective dimension that is meant to terrify. In this world, no holds are barred and nothing is sacred. In its constant violation of boundaries it matches the limitlessly intrusive character of unregulated global capitalism itself in daily life, in which anything is up for grabs. Virtually anyone and anything are a target: Barack Obama's nationality. Or, during Trump's campaign, *New York Times* journalist Serge Kovaleski's disability, Federal Judge Gonzalo Curiel's ethnicity, vulnerable Trump University students' private financial hopes and fears, or Hillary Clinton's physical safety.

When feeling threatened, Trump will lash out at Republican politicians and conservative commentators, putting them on notice: Paul Ryan ("very weak"), Lindsay Graham ("very sad"), Rand Paul ("didn't get the right gene"), Glenn Beck ("mental basket case"), former Fox News host Megyn Kelly ("blood coming out of her whatever"), and most recently, MSNBC *Morning Joe* cohost Mika Brzezinski ("low I.Q. Crazy Mika").[81]

Even media moguls who helped build Trump's brand and launch his campaign, like CNN's CEO Jeff Zucker, aren't spared ("failed @NBC and now failing @CNN"). Practicing the one-way loyalty of tyrannical CEOs, he doesn't hesitate to publicly undercut a cabinet member like Jeff Sessions for recusing himself from the Russian investigations or disparage Senate Majority Leader Mitch McConnell for failing to pass Trumpcare. As it is with Trump as boss, so it is with Trump the politician: he never answers criticisms, he simply launches new attacks. Challenged, he does what he has always done in contentious business dealings, he simply countersues. Offense is everything—even in the dangerous arena of foreign and military affairs, such as responding to North Korea's quickly advancing international ballistic missile program. Relentlessly expansive and seeking out new targets, bullies and violent aggressors like him are extremist and arbitrary by necessity. How does he meet a demand for accountability? With further disrespect of the target. As we've seen, in the case of Megyn Kelly it takes the form of paternal advice to toughen up: "But you gotta get over it. Fight back, do whatever you have to do." Or in the case of Hillary Clinton, who belittled his foreign policy proposals, the form of an outright threat of her arrest and incarceration should he become president, or later, assassination should *she* be elected and not him.[82] You either enter Trump's world on his terms and follow his script, or you're out. That is, you're fired or, in a new twist, put behind bars or even killed.

However, like many political attack ads that preceded Trump's entry into politics, to achieve his ends Trump doesn't always need to destroy his opponent, but simply to dishonor or paralyze her or him and introduce a doubt in the minds of the audience. And Trump is free to abandon a position or statement on a whim—such is his privilege and power—as when he claimed that his advocacy of a ban on all Muslims entering the U.S. was "just a suggestion," an opening negotiating position or bid. Which he can then return to and double down on, as he did after the Orlando terrorist mass shooting in June 2016.

Many of his aggressive smears take the passive-aggressive form of hearsay or rumors that he is merely "reporting," qualified by "So I am told," or "Some say so but I don't know." What's paramount is to grab the limelight and define the debate. The content is often less important than the preemptive violence and excess that intimidate rivals and awe audiences.

Trump even uses his own contradictory statements to his advantage: they create an ambiguity that confuses opponents. Like the opportunist populist leaders of far-right movements described by Paxton, Trump's behavior during the campaign and after he assumed office follows no coherent program or ideology—nor apparently does it always need to—other than the expression of the pure free energy and forward movement of his entitled self in defense of a declining America and its embattled middle and working classes.[83] And as the primaries and elections progressed, Trump's violent, arbitrary personal style became the very content of his campaign and, later on, of his administration.

Government as Family Business

Trump treats political issues—and politics generally—like his business holdings: contractors, employees, clients, allies, and family members are assets to be manipulated—and abused. This is the force and freedom of a family businessman and fully entrepreneurial politician. By the end of the presidential campaign, when repugnant details of his business and personal dealings had come to light and reached the general public, what provoked revulsion may also have stimulated perverse fascination with the fact that, despite his sordid past and multiple bankruptcies that would have destroyed common mortals like ourselves, Trump not only magically survived but *flourished.*

On the edge of financial ruin in 1990, he pivoted, putting less and less of his own money into business ventures, and simply licensed his brand to hotels bearing his name, which followed the march of globalization around the planet. This is one of the takeaways from a cursory read of Wayne Barrett's biography, aptly titled *Trump: The Greatest Show on Earth.* In this regard Trump's ties to the Russian government and oligarchs and possible money laundering through his real estate holdings can perhaps best be understood by viewing Trump as first and foremost an unscrupulous businessman whose many murky business deals some of which involve German and Russian private and state banks, go back thirty years. And, in 2016, Russian business partners may have offered him a deal in hacked political information that in his mind he couldn't refuse.

By March 2016 Trump had taken the next step: he graduated from verbal bullying to frequent calls to physical violence towards protestors at his rallies. Far from slowing his relentless rise in the polls, Trump seemed to legitimatize a vein of violence in the public sphere that had begun to feed on itself. He had edged closer to a truly pre-fascist political style that is aggrieved, xenophobic, nostalgic, paranoid, and physically violent. Beyond the law and its routine protections. And successful enough to secure him an Electoral College victory. He expressed not only many voters' fears and grievances of living in an unstable market economy and fifteen years of war but also a public culture of intimidation and bullying that silently legitimizes the most authoritarian behavior and policies.

As I've said before, Trump's populist genius has been at once to personify all that unfettered capitalism promises and to lead a revolt against all its disappointments in the name of those very same promises. [84] Many (including this writer) thought that this contradiction might explode before Election Day if, for example, the Trump University scandal, which revealed him to have shamelessly exploited financially vulnerable white consumers for personal gain, didn't go away. No longer admiring spectators of Trump's bullying of others, his populist base might identify with his victims and hand him his pink slip.

At that juncture, another hope was that perhaps Trump's greatest enemy wouldn't be so much his shady business deals, the Democratic Party, or the hostile media but rather the overly long, dysfunctional U.S. election cycle. It can sap even the most robust and powerful campaign that under a different electoral system might perhaps have already put Trump in office. Even Donald Trump, Cyberbully and King of the Tweet, might suffer overexposure from the 24/7 media. But none of those scenarios came to pass. In his case, apparently, there is no such thing as too much publicity—it is what he craves rather than fears (except perhaps when it comes to his business dealings with foreign entities or parties), for he thrives on it as a majority of voters discovered on November 8th.

If the success of GOP skullduggery, from voter suppression initiatives and gerrymandering to then FBI Director James Comey's interference, didn't answer the question nagging voters during the primaries and fall campaign about what was in store for them Election Night, newly elected Trump made more than clear the meaning of his victory. That day, with the eyes of the nation upon him, he pointedly did not issue the traditional reassurance to those who did not vote for him that he was the president of all Americans. Rather, we were given to understand, he was now the president of *his* people and the CEO of the nation. And that those who voted against him were disenfranchised and dismissed.

The Political Synergy of Trump's Multiple Identities

Trump was uniquely poised to carry out an insurgent run for the White House in a time of popular discontent and coarsened public life. His violent personality traits were socially rooted and enabled by his status as head of a family real estate business in New York and by the legitimacy conferred upon tyrannical CEOs by new management models and the business press. He projected a potent multifaceted image, unmatched by any other candidate but that drew on some of the deepest wellsprings of contemporary U.S. culture: successful, unscrupulous entrepreneur, financially and politically independent, economic populist, global brand, reckless bully persona, media-savvy celebrity, purveyor of global glitz, old-fashioned paternalist, political outsider, and potential strongman.

He is a uniquely hybrid figure of political authority, whose qualities taken separately would not have afforded him the aura of power and impunity he enjoyed throughout his career and the recent election cycle. Without his global brand, as simply a successful businessman, he would not have enjoyed politically advantageous wide name recognition and remained, fatally, just another political outsider; or lacking wealth and financial independence, he would never have been able to come forward as a paternal "savior CEO" to challenge the political establishments of both parties.

Absent his bad-boy glamour and celebrity status, his crass bully persona and unscrupulous business practices would have wrecked his candidacy.[85] Without his populist attacks on free trade and the outsourcing of jobs overseas, his racist and misogynist attitudes would have cut short his bid for the White House. Finally, if he weren't a successful tyrannical CEO, his authoritarian political style would have been only so much macho bluster and exerted little attraction upon voters. Concentrated together in the same person, however, Trump's personal attributes created a synergy that helped propel him to the White House. As such, Trump's example offers a dark lesson on how deep currents of capitalist culture can upend the electoral politics of a liberal democracy in crisis.

After Trump: Entrepreneurialism and Authoritarian Political Rule

So whether or not Trump and congressional Republicans successfully implement their counterrevolution to remake the federal government as we know it, it is crucial to remember that the enabling social and economic conditions of his rise will remain in place. And should Trump and his allies fail or lose control of Congress in 2018, many voters will await the emergence of another aggressive capitalist folk hero and defiant white man. A corporate "savior" like Trump, he (not she) will be granted every indulgence, every reprieve—and will be most likely not from New York and discredited Wall Street but from Silicon Valley, in the form of a charismatic, libertarian, but younger and less brazenly self-interested and contemptuous CEO, venture capitalist, or hedge fund manager, who will advocate some version of "corporate despotism...a little Steve Jobs here, a little Ayn Rand there, and some Ray Kurzweil for color."[86]

CHAPTER FOUR

Political Thuggery and Party Identities

Crucial to understanding the longer history of intimidation in electoral politics are the GOP's and Democratic Party's different internal cultures of identity, loyalty, and governing, as well as the social composition of their respective members. With this in mind I pick up the thread of Republican actions and Democratic responses begun in Chapter One, and now extend it up through the verbal and physical threats issued against Barack Obama and other Democratic politicians by political adversaries during Obama's terms of office.

A Restructured Democratic Party and Its Cautious Strategies

Democratic leaders' weak responses to the Republican theft of the 2000 presidential elections and the smearing of Max Cleland and John Kerry in subsequent political races hardly stand alone in the recent history of the party. Already in 1988 Republican operative Lee Atwater's notoriously racist Willie Horton ad campaign, featuring the image of a Massachusetts black man who committed a brutal rape while on furlough, caught the Democratic candidate Michael Dukakis (governor of Massachusetts) off guard and went largely without a response. It is as if the Democratic Party, which had invented the political attack ad in 1960 (with the false claims of a "missile gap" with the Soviet Union) and 1964 (with the anti-Goldwater "Daisy" ad warning of imminent nuclear war), by the end of the Reagan years (1980-88) had lost its knack for effective televised messaging and ceded to the opposing party the terrain of broadcast and cable media.

Citing George McGovern's disastrous 1972 antiwar presidential campaign, party leaders in 1984 established superdelegates of elected officials and party chairs to mitigate the influence of discontented voters in presidential primaries. And after liberal Walter Mondale's landslide loss to an aging

Ronald Reagan that same year, younger leaders like Bill Clinton (the so-called New Democrats or "neoliberals") founded the centrist Democratic Leadership Council (DLC) that adopted the new Beltway consensus supporting conservative fiscal policies. In essence, establishment Democrats largely ceded the field of public discourse to the apologists for free-market solutions and small government, with few opposing voices to make the case for public services.

Arguably it was at that time Democratic leaders sought refuge in well-organized voter turnout initiatives and the closed-door world of policymaking, whose fact-based discourse expressing liberal good intentions presumably spoke for itself to voters. This was when centrist Democrats followed Bill Clinton's lead in "triangulating" between liberal and conservative politics in the hopes of attracting moderate suburban voters, and the subsequent fetishization of "compromise" became party doctrine. As we shall see in this chapter and the next devoted to the 2016 elections, this helped shape an entire political identity. One has the impression that the Democratic leadership somehow felt that the momentum of the fifty years of congressional domination Democrats enjoyed since the time of FDR would still carry the day in a more conservative political environment and protect the legacy of the New Deal and the Civil Rights movement and their underlying assumptions about government's place in ordinary people's lives. In this view, even in the absence of charismatic candidates, no further vigorous defense or even education of the public about what government can do to promote individual and general welfare was required.

Thanks to Bernie Sanders's powerful 2016 presidential bid, it is now clearer than ever that under the leadership of the Democratic National Committee (DNC) and the newly formed Democratic Leadership Council, by the late 1990s Democratic Party centrist politics had dropped any meaningful mobilization of its liberal base. Instead it focused on presidential campaigns and a reliance on big corporate donors to finance them, thereby initiating the long neglect of the nitty-gritty of local politics and citizen involvement in issues closest to home.

Gone, too, were the strains of economic populism. This also reflected the diminishing presence of trade union members among the party's rank and file and leadership, and the defection of many of them (the so-called Reagan Democrats) to the GOP. The party's core constituencies (later called "firewalls") were taken for granted and were called upon only every four years to take action in the voting booth.

In the absence of other forms of sustained political organizing and education, such as that afforded by trade unions (already in steep decline), this would prove to be catastrophic in the long run, especially in congressional and local races. However, despite party leaders' best efforts, the energy and the commitment of the base did not vanish, as Howard Dean's and Barack Obama's anti–Iraq War candidacies, through their appeal to young voters and the novel creation of small donor, Internet-based networks, made clear in 2004 and 2008.[87]

A supreme irony was that, despite their new reliance on policymaking, in general Democrats did not fare all that well in framing national issues. For, ever since the landslide defeat of Barry Goldwater in 1964, conservative Republicans had been patiently building a new intellectual infrastructure. It consisted of well-financed foundations and think-tanks that developed hundreds of new policy papers advocating libertarian and neo-conservative positions, sponsored workshops to recruit students and journalists, and fielded a new phalanx of spokesmen and women that began to populate TV news programs.[88]

The Republicans created a relentless drumbeat on talk shows and in the news media that outmatched whatever Democrats could muster on a daily basis, and translated the arcane prose of conservative policy into memorable sound-bites, an art that to this day still escapes most Democratic Party leaders. Bill Clinton and Barack Obama would prove to be the memorable exceptions that confirmed the rule: without a magnetic leader as their spokesperson, cautious, centrist politics remained quite vulnerable to spirited attacks. And in Obama's case his considerable oratorical talents were used sparingly, and were unable to assuage accumulated voter anxiety during his two terms.

The Advent of Obama and the Rise of the Tea Party

The invasion of Iraq that provoked new liberal and progressive mobilization also opened cracks in the media's conservative consensus in the form of Jon Stewart's late-night *Daily Show* on Comedy Central and Keith Olbermann's evening news program, *Countdown with Keith Olbermann*, on MSNBC. The new energy helped drive Obama's insurgent candidacy, which had started outside the orbit of the DNC and ran on the themes of "hope" and national reconciliation that explicitly rejected the divisive, fear-based politics that had dominated the United States for many decades, especially during the George W. Bush administration. The charismatic black candidate's speeches set off an enthusiastic response among young voters, baffling established political commentators, and in the eyes of many observers, Obama seemed to herald a turning point in recent U.S. political history. However, Obama's victory in 2008 did not mark a reprieve from the harsher tone of public discourse, nor did his call for a politics of respect turn back the tide of political intimidation, especially that of Democrats by Republicans.[89]

On the contrary, with the election of the first black president political bullying reached new heights as Republican opponents and media celebrities, such as Fox News host Glenn Beck and CNN's Lou Dobbs, launched campaigns targeting not only the new president's policies but also his very person in a bid to destabilize his presidency— everything from calling him a racist (anti-white) and questioning his place of birth (seconded by Donald Trump) to claiming Obama would take citizens' guns away from them and calling for armed resistance against the new administration.

The Tea Party, financed by the Koch Brothers, went so far as to hold rallies close to official town hall meetings hosted by Obama on the proposed Affordable Care Act, at which in Arizona and New Hampshire radical right members showed up with loaded weapons. It was a potent reminder, if ever one was needed, that many of the accumulated 300 million guns in the U.S.—twice as many as in 1968—had a purpose other than personal enjoyment, one that was profoundly political and served as a silent—and not so silent—form of intimidation of political opponents.[90]

Two years later, in January 2011, the threat of armed violence culminated in the mass shooting by a gunman who targeted a staunch defender of the Affordable Care Act, Congresswoman Gabrielle Giffords (D-AZ), at an outdoor meeting with her constituents, and left her severely wounded and six other people dead. The assassination attempt came after a hard-fought electoral campaign in which her opponent Jesse Kelly, an ex-Marine and Tea Party member, distributed flyers calling for voters to come out to a meeting and shoot an assault rifle to support him in defeating Giffords ("Get on Target for Victory in November Help remove Gabrielle Giffords from office Shoot a fully-automatic M16 with Jesse Kelly" [sic]). During the same election, former Republican vice-presidential candidate Sarah Palin had even featured an electoral map of congressional districts of Democratic members of Congress, including Giffords, who had voted for the Affordable Care Act, with crosshairs of a gunsight superimposed on each district. After the shooting Palin remained defiantly unapologetic.

Democrats responded as did Republicans, by denouncing the attack as a national tragedy and issuing calls for the cooling of political rhetoric, as if both parties were equally culpable. Bipartisanship won the day at the expense of clear-eyed analysis. The local sheriff overseeing the investigation, Clarence W. Dupnik, had no such qualms and demonstrated an understanding of how political intimidation can work to incite unstable citizens:

There's reason to believe that this individual may have a mental issue. And I think people who are unbalanced are especially susceptible to vitriol. People tend to pooh-pooh this business about all the vitriol we hear inflaming the American public by people who make a living off of doing that. That may be free speech, but it's not without consequences.

When you look at unbalanced people, how they respond to the vitriol that comes out of certain mouths about tearing down the government. The anger, the hatred, the bigotry that goes on in this country is getting to be outrageous.[91]

2010: Demobilizing Democrats

Election Night and Inauguration Day witnessed the largest public assemblies in recent U.S. election history—250,000 in Chicago's Hyde Park to greet the victorious Obama, and 1.8 million on the Washington Mall to watch him take the oath of office. One would think that would have constituted a unique political advantage over Republicans demoralized and panicked by their electoral losses. Indeed, Obama seemed poised to exploit his political leverage when he named as his chief of staff fellow Chicagoan Rahm Emmanuel, a fierce Democratic partisan and political brawler.

Emmanuel's appointment was taken by many as a warning shot to the opposing party, as if to say "Don't mess with me," and a sign that Obama was preparing to do battle. But that was not to be. Perhaps thrown, or even frightened, by political pressure represented by the huge outpouring of public enthusiasm his very campaign elicited and received and the high expectations it raised, once in office Obama busily worked to return to politics as usual behind closed doors and away from the streets, demobilizing his massive number of supporters.

What's more, far from applying his hardball tactics to fend off the Republican onslaught and obstructionism, Emmanuel instead targeted liberal Democratic members of Congress and devoted his energies to blocking their demands for implementing a progressive agenda that would address voter discontent. The issues were many, from rapidly winding down the Iraq War, curtailing the excesses of the Patriot Act, and prosecuting those responsible for illegal measures of exception in the War on Terror to rescinding the Bush tax cuts for the wealthy. They also included assisting millions of homeowners who were victims of mortgage fraud, investigating those implicated in the great financial scandals (Enron, Iraq, the post–Hurricane Katrina cleanup in New Orleans, etc.), and restoring financial regulation in the wake of the 2008 financial collapse.

Not only did Wall Street malfeasance go unpunished but also many top bankers and CEOs enjoyed a seat at Obama's table, from which representatives of traditional Democratic constituencies were conspicuously absent.[92] He made his own fiscally conservative calls for austerity, and appointed in 2010 the Simpson-Bowles Commission, dominated by advocates of small government and cutting entitlement and safety-net programs like Social Security and Medicare.

Insurgent candidate from outside the DNC though he was, the inexperienced Obama, contending with the financial crisis and the daily demands of governing, soon underwent what sociologists call "institutional capture" by the Beltway establishment and its priorities.[93] "Hope" became a milquetoast identity rather than a robust political program.

The political fallout was swift and immediate: in the 2010 midterm elections disappointed Democrats and Independents stayed home, the record turnout of black voters in 2008 plummeted, and the Republicans won a record sixty additional seats in the House and four governorships in Pennsylvania and the old industrial Midwest—a warning of things to come—which gave them the unparalleled opportunity to gerrymander in their favor dozens of congressional districts thanks to the 2010 Census.[94] The liberal political momentum of 2008 was broken, and Republicans redoubled their campaign of intimidation and obstruction.

Obama's response to GOP actions mirrored that of leaders of his party before: largely to ignore them. Committed to the public strategy of hopeful bipartisanship and compromise, a weakened Obama was even less prepared for the renewed attacks and continued to achieve few results for his efforts (the Affordable Care Act was passed without Republican support in 2010 by Democratic majorities in Congress).

Matters soon reached such a pass that the serene and unflappable bearing that had served him so well in 2008 to reassure worried voters during the financial crisis and the debates with John McCain now worked against Obama and his allies. However calm and reasonable he was in demeanor, he was now seen as detached and indifferent, and even viewed as the aggressor and the bully in the eyes of the aggrieved crowds and their right-wing sponsors. This is a good example of "felt" or affective politics at its most powerful. This was something that, unfortunately, escaped most Democratic politicians and liberal commentators, who contented themselves with pointing out the obvious lies and misrepresentations.

What they failed to realize is that what was at hand was an open-ended preemptive campaign of verbal and physical aggression and bullying whose real goal was less to convince people of "facts" than to seize control of public discourse and sow doubt and confusion in the minds of a fearful public.

Party Loyalty, Social Identity, and Cultures of Governing

Among Democratic and Republican establishment leaders there are active cultures of loyalty that are tightly bound to political and social identities that in turn shape their respective concepts of governing and national campaign strategies. In the case of Democrats their identity appears to be largely one based on a self-image, defined by a political record of generous or liberal good intentions and an adherence to ethical principles that requires little in the way of new translation and fresh political messaging by candidates to the larger voting public beyond what a charismatic voice can do. In this view, Democrats have been and are simply "good people," whose good works should command voters' loyalty and gratitude. Just look at their record since the New Deal, or more recently, the legacy of the Clinton and Obama administrations!

How else to explain in federal elections (if not the primaries) Democrats' historical distaste for hardball politics and reluctance to descend into the ring and respond in kind to Republican attacks that target precisely the Democrats' lofty self-image and identity? The preferred method is to impugn Democrats' motives and intentions through innuendo, an approach that has the advantage of forgoing the necessity of adducing proof and difficult to refute.

This has been a fundamental political vulnerability for Democrats over the last thirty years. Paradoxically, this self-image on the national stage clashes with that of local Democrats, who throughout the twentieth century excelled in the rough-and-tumble politics of urban and state politics, perhaps because, unlike at the national level, the benefits of political victory are so immediate and tangible (better schools, transportation, and refuse collection, access to municipal and state government jobs, etc.).[95]

Shaping these practices of loyalty and identity is the respective social composition of each party. And here we observe that political loyalty actually entails not one but two components: first, an internal one to the party and then, a second one to the institutions of government. The Republican establishment, today still very white, moneyed, and majority Protestant, operates as an exclusive country club whose members practice a ruling class's discipline and form of loyalty that put Democrats to shame. They seem to flow naturally from Republicans' more homogenous social composition, though the rise of the Tea Party and Trump's triumph in the primaries have stimulated talk of establishing superdelegates along the lines of the Democratic Party in order to dilute direct party member input in the selection of a presidential nominee.

Loyalty has generally served the GOP well: after internal squabbles, GOP leaders almost always fall back in line. (Look how quickly Republican politicians—if not commentators—

lined up behind Trump after a spectacularly brutal primary season.) They even practice a form of *omertà* that keeps their sex scandals in-house and largely out of the public eye; rare is the woman who goes public with kiss-and-tell stories. Moreover, Republicans have a proprietary relationship to government: they think they own it, or if they don't, think they *should*. This is the very measure of their elitism (and tempers what nationalist impulses they may have—more about which below).

They act as if they were raised not only to govern but, as full-throated capitalists, to *rule over* others. Born in the anterooms of power, they do not have to demonstrate their citizenship or patriotism, nor does the public demand it of them. Such is the special status afforded them by the American free-market culture that respects wealth and success. If anything, their displays of raw patriotism often serve as a cover to their abiding self-interest more than anything else. Accountable to no one other than their own kind, as owners and senior executives they view rules and regulations as written for others rather than as applying to themselves, especially when they feel their interests threatened.

They are the very embodiment and force of a capitalist entitlement that promotes a populist discourse of personal fulfillment and social mobility through individual initiative, aggressive entrepreneurship, and free markets untrammeled by government—a discourse to which many Americans subscribe—and combines it with class privilege. Borne along by the larger society, Republican leaders' sense of entitlement is the envy of many ordinary citizens and residents.

So Republicans don't always see their interests served by active government, and their loyalty remains primarily to themselves and less to the nation as such. In national politics, they, unlike Democrats, don't always seek popular validation—their sense of self is independent of politics and precedes it. Like Machiavelli's Prince, for them winning is everything, and they accept being feared rather than loved. So rewriting the rules of procedure or decorum and shifting the goalposts to keep opponents off balance are all in a day's work. Examples include: the Supreme Court Republican majority's decision to intervene in state election processes (2000 Florida vote recount); the invitation to a head of state to address Congress behind the back of the White House (Netanyahu); the unprecedented nine-month-long refusal to consider Obama's Supreme Court nominee Merrick Garland and one hundred other obstructed federal judicial nominations; advancing major legislation without prior committee hearings (Trumpcare); undercutting congressional investigations (of Russian electoral meddling); defaming the Congressional Budget Office; etc.

When given the chance, Republicans have no qualms in breaking the rules, starting in the earliest days of the Cold War when they turned President Truman's anti-communist crusade and loyalty program into a wave of rabid red-baiting (McCarthyism) against Democrats, the New Deal, and federal agencies, 96 and later when they launched in 1968 the "Southern strategy" of fanning the flames of white voters' fears.

These aggressive tactics continued up through the impeachment of Bill Clinton in 1999 and the stolen election in 2000. Today it extends to voter suppression initiatives and the interference in the presidential campaign by then FBI Director James Comey and former New York City mayor Rudolph Giuliani. Often this has involved delegating the most unsavory tasks to political operatives (Lee Atwater and Karl Rove's lieutenants), rogue politicians (Joseph McCarthy), political action committees (Swift Boat Veterans for Truth), and other third parties like Super PACS. Of late, however, publicly dropping the velvet glove comes more and more easily to them. The mailed fist is visible for those who have eyes to see.

Democrats, on the other hand, are an economically, ethnically, and racially composite group that is publicly fractious and poorly disciplined. To be sure, many are very entitled—they want and expect many things—but most can't be said to have been raised since birth confident that government and management of the fate of others and of the entire nation were their destiny. Mastery of their own fate, defiantly, yes; mastery of the fate of others, less so. At the same time they seem to express the hope and belief that national political institutions and their rules (including laws) will protect them and guarantee political enfranchisement.[97]

Their loyalty to the federal government more than matches their loyalty to the party, but it is a nervous one. Democrats seem to embody the almost middle-class sense of propriety of the upwardly mobile, anxiously seeking recognition of their new-found status that their Republican opponents rarely grant them: they are often viewed as so many barbarians within the gates and treated as such. Moreover, as liberal or reform-minded capitalists, party leaders—even as they practice greater loyalty to federal institutions—operate more from the ideological margins of the free-market economic system, and thus from a position that is experienced as less legitimate.[98]

Certainly Republicans have always thought so, and since the 1950s they have made it clear through political smears and red-baiting of Democrats, especially during the Cold War. (Which goes to show that political intimidation of this kind has always had more to do with delegitimizing domestic opponents than with combatting a foreign menace.) So here we face a political paradox: often viewed with disdain by Republicans as less than mainstream and "American," Democrats practice a deeper loyalty to the nation-state and its federal institutions than their opponents, who see themselves as true nationals but express increasing contempt for the welfare of the nation and its government.

Less secure in their social and ideological status, certain Democrats act as if they still seek acceptance by their abusive social and ideological betters, an acceptance that will never come. It's like looking for love in all the wrong places. Reticent before the necessity of dirtying themselves publicly and compromising their status as accredited players, they have come to prefer managing politics at a safe hygienic distance through hopeful bipartisanship, the strength of their detailed policy initiatives based on large data aggregates, and voter turnout drives. They dropped the adversarial politics of economic populism dating from the New Deal that in the past drew lines between themselves and Republicans in concrete terms, such that they matched the Republicans' "us-them" strategy of political smears and red-baiting that attempted to delegitimize Democrats and their policies and ostracize them from the national political arena.

Jeopardizing their fragile legitimacy by engaging in hardball politics is now considered by most Democrats as too risky—or so it would appear. Content with their self-image and identity, they forget that elections are not popularity contests but rather bids for power and that to the victor go both the spoils and control of the public narrative. Winning bestows its own rewards: more often than not, victory makes right, so to speak, not the reverse. Trump, entrepreneur turned politician, never forgets this.

Arguably all these factors contributed to undermine Democrats' resolve in responding to Republican acts of intimidation and skullduggery over the last thirty years. In the case of Hillary Clinton, what stands out in her run for president was her stunning inability to anticipate her own vulnerability to potential attacks even when, in the cases of the hacked campaign and DNC emails, possession of a private email server while Secretary of State, and the dysfunctional actions and relationships of the DNC and campaign staff, she had been in possession of the facts for many months.

Victim of a strange passivity (*What was she waiting for?*), she did nothing to preempt the aggressive assaults and damaging revelations to come and seize the initiative by airing the troubling emails early on and firing staff before she was forced to, both of which would have worked to her advantage. She seemed more courageous at confronting Trump than in cleaning house and renewing Democratic Party echelons. What she mainly did was to invoke principles and precedents of one kind or another in defense of her actions and those of her colleagues, as if she counted on the goodwill of public opinion to exonerate her from Republicans' outlandish charges and the embarrassing details of confidential correspondence.

Her campaign seemed to deem her credentials sufficient to carry her to victory and to bank on the expectation that Trump's bullying personality would seal the election in her favor. In so doing she fatally underestimated the unforgiving political climate in which she had to operate, a climate, however, with which she was all too familiar since her earliest days as First Lady.[99]

Donald Trump's Identity and Aggression: He Meant What He Said

Donald Trump broke with the practices and self-images of both parties. Nominally and expediently Republican, he has none of the GOP leaders' loyalty to the party and even less of their sense of discipline and discretion. He is the attack dog become master. When it comes of acts of intimidation and violence, he outdoes them in every way and won't hesitate to heap abuse upon his putative allies. He also discarded the old Republican elitism for a fiercely white nationalist posture that echoed isolationist strains in international affairs that the GOP establishment had abandoned decades earlier in favor of committing the U.S. to a policy of maintaining spheres of influence abroad.[100]

What Trump does share is the Republicans' instrumentalization of government for private gain and their cynical disregard for rules and regulations, but again, unlike the GOP old guard and like the vulgar tabloid politician that he is, he makes no secret of it. It is his version of transparency and brutally so, to the thrill of his rebellious supporters. Trump may be a private-school-educated WASP born to wealth, but he is also a second-generation American with little patience for the niceties of good manners and establishment hypocrisy. Capitalist folk hero, he is the captivating embodiment of the defiant, mythical free-born white man openly hostile to government and people who depend on it.

His aggressive liberty in word and deed, unconstrained by party, the dignity of office, or social and ethical principles, is what many voters admire and identify with. In other words, Trump's violence—including his brazen self-interest—is the very token of his liberty and trustworthiness. It is not incidental to his politics but central to its content. The violence is the message. Under Trump, Republicans' cynical use of government may have reached a new stage, in which the state risks becoming simply the instrument of lawless repression. Certainly that it is one of the takeaways from Trump's pardon of convicted former Arizona sheriff Joe Arpaio, who had used his office to terrorize the Latino and immigrant communities.

Trump marks the culmination of the steady resurgence of the expression of violent personal and collective sovereignty over others in U.S. daily life and politics in the figure of the sadistic strongman. [101] Since becoming the Republican nominee he has worked to replace the GOP's culture of loyalty to the party and its establishment with a personal culture of loyalty to himself. In this regard, Trump did mean what he said, and many voters responded. This is the dark information that Democrats failed to factor into their electoral thinking. Thus, as in the 2000 presidential election, late in the night on Election Day the majority of those who voted were served once again the spectacle of their own political disenfranchisement and treated as so many expendable employees by the political system.

CHAPTER FIVE

Playing for Keeps: The 2016 Elections

The Abusive Entrepreneur Enters Politics

As I hope it is now clear, Donald Trump's electoral ascent in 2016 can be understood as the climax of a recent U.S. history of political intimidation and violence, revolutions in cable and social media, and the concurrent rise of aggressive talk radio and reality TV, as well as of the simmering populist discontent stemming from the stresses of working in globalized economies and living in a state of war since 9/11.[102]

Many reasons explain Trump's Electoral College victory and Hillary Clinton's defeat, but at its most crude, the outcome was a replay of the 2000 elections, which saw political intimidation of poll workers in Florida and unremitting partisanship by Florida's Secretary of State and Republican members of the U.S. Supreme Court put George Bush in the White House. This time around it was hackers of DNC and Clinton campaign email accounts and then FBI Director James Comey, along with voter suppression initiatives in key states, that did the dirty work.[103]

Equally important was Trump the candidate: reckless bully persona, he capitalized on the aura of the rogue entrepreneur/tyrannical CEO as capitalist folk hero in a society still in thrall to the free market and brilliantly exploited his status as global brand, political outsider, and symbol of change.[104] Like three-time prime minister Silvio Berlusconi in post–Cold War Italy, he brought to the world of U.S. politics and its isolated, aging party organizations his peerless mastery of cable TV, tabloid news, and the cult of celebrity. He broke new ground in using the power of social media to communicate directly with voters over the heads of mainstream media outlets and the apparatuses of established elites and their political parties that had served as the traditional brokers and gatekeepers of the national conversation and higher office.[105] Wresting control of the content and rhythm of the 24/7 news cycle by a new outrageous tweet every day, he received $5.8 billion in free media, vastly expanding the reach and scope of his persona and message.[106] He rewrote the script of political campaigning and emptied public debate and political reporting of meaningful substance.

With Trump, cyberbullying made its formal entrance into national politics. By virtue of his verbal taunts and threats of physical violence, he took to another level the culture of public intimidation, fear, and counterfactuality as instruments of power that George Bush, Dick Cheney, and Donald Rumsfeld had first deployed so effectively. At present in Washington and New York, Trump is rewriting the script of *governing*, and the battle is joined between the new regime and media organizations and the apparatuses of the political elites and their parties over who will be the reliable source of news and information and who gets to define and enact the national agenda.

As I wrote previously, Trump also stood as the raw expression of the Republicans' decades-long "Southern strategy" of exploiting working- and middle-class white voters' fears in the face of economic uncertainty, stagnating wages, and changing populations affecting key regions. Taking up the racist strategies that were first coded in euphemisms ("law & order," "crime," "War on Drugs," etc.) forty years ago and then outsourced more recently to the Tea Party's very public but still politically marginal manifestations, where they received their rawest expression, Trump proceeded in turn to mainstream them in their new, overt form and make them a central part of his public bid for office and now of his new administration. In a sense, Trump has completed the process of converting campaigning through intimidation and fearmongering into a form of governing begun sixteen years ago under George W. Bush.

Hillary Clinton's Unflinching Campaign

To her credit, Hillary Clinton, perhaps encouraged by the example of Elizabeth Warren and Bernie Sanders, did show an understanding of the danger posed, not only by Trump's right-wing populist message, but also by his very *methods*, which legitimize authoritarian behavior and policies. In the face of threats to her very person (incarceration and assassination) she did not flinch, and in the debates and her political ads she stood up to his abusive and disrespectful outbursts and successfully baited him with facts and stories about his shabby treatment of employees and vendors, members of communities of color, women, and his nonpayment of federal taxes, thereby reassuring her base and stopping the slippage of her lead in the polls.

Clinton was attempting to rework the older, timid Democratic script, while Trump radicalized the old Republican one based on perceptions of "character" and appeals to fear. But in the end, it would appear that her defiant "facts" and mockery of his dysfunctional personality enjoyed only limited reach outside of liberal circles. What's more, her tactic may have actually caused a backlash among hesitant voters, when they were reprised by a mainstream news media that, as Glenn Greenwald reminded us after the election, is the second most distrusted American institution after Congress.[107] Clinton's message, as hard-hitting as it was, remained prisoner of Trump's themes or narrative "frames" (as linguist George Lakoff would say) and was too focused on Trump's character and not enough on solutions to issues voters cared about passionately.

Last but not least, the message was hampered by the messenger: going into the campaign, Clinton, like Trump, had historically high disapproval ratings, but they were judged by different standards, not only because of their gender but also because, unlike him, she was the very symbol of the political establishment and opportunist politicians. As unfair as it may seem, in a contest of character Clinton was fated to lose, for rogue Trump's flaws—violent narcissist, brutal CEO, and unapologetic racist and misogynist—were viewed by many as *virtues*, or at the very least without consequence, focused as they were on his populist and anti-elitist message.

Just as important, Clinton possessed none of Trump's charisma—not that of a politician, but of the decisive (white) male CEO and entrepreneur, fearless risk-taker, breaker of furniture to get things done, etc.—which had won him indulgence on the part of many voters even as the repugnant details of his business dealings and private life came to light. Voters were not so forgiving of the overly cautious Clinton. An instinctual incrementalist to boot, Clinton was a poor vehicle for the Democratic Party platform's new populist line in favor of free college tuition, the fifteen-dollar minimum wage, student debt relief, Medicare expansion, etc.

Finally, it must be said that in the end Clinton remained true to the internal culture of the Democratic Party establishment, which since the 1980s has prized technical policymaking over political messaging and mobilization (except through a charismatic candidate), recourse to large donors, and survey-based polling data. [108] Cautious management of its socially diverse base led to reliance on static group-defined "firewalls" (women, Blacks, Latinos, union households) whose votes are routinely taken for granted, a ground game focused on voter turnout initiatives, and faith that demographic shifts trending Democratic would automatically translate into meaningful votes. However, it is now apparent that Clinton lost to Trump 28% of the Latino vote and up to 45% of the union vote, while African-American turnout was low in key battleground states.[109]

Clinton's and the Democrats' campaign strategy could be said to betray a fundamental commitment of energies and resources to a narrow strategy of internal party *control* and predictable electoral outcomes. It was not an expansive, risk-taking approach but rather one based on a zero-sum model of political authority or capital that is always viewed as prone to atrophy: if you share it, you lose it. Additional investments and expenditures in the way of opening up party echelons to new blood, adopting new ideological frames or themes, or pursuing new strategies can only deplete it, never increase it. Political capital must be saved for a future time, a time that is always deferred and rarely materializes. [110] This is the underlying philosophy of political incrementalism.

The tumultuous 2016 primaries and presidential campaign revealed this strategy for what it was: too abstract, ill-informed, and unresponsive to changing circumstances. It led to a disastrous neglect of an Electoral College strategy targeting key regions (most notoriously the depressed rural industrial areas of the Midwest, a region with a new phalanx of Republican-dominated statehouses and governorships but where Bernie Sanders did well). The strategy gave no consideration to the possibility that a controversial candidate like Trump might compromise the reliability of polling that took voters' responses largely at their word and did not count first-time voters. [111] This abstract perspective plagued liberal commentators outside of the campaign as well.

For example, Nobel Prize–winning economist and *New York Times* columnist Paul Krugman, otherwise clear-eyed about the political effectiveness of Republican scorched-earth tactics and the power of mainstream news media to hollow out meaningful political reporting, was equally flummoxed and tweeted his electoral shock: "This is not my country!" However, perhaps the country never was his, or rather, was never fully taken into account by his own data analysis, which created large optimistic aggregates concerning employment growth under Obama and the net gain of jobs due to NAFTA. Moreover, his analysis overlooked specifics such as the increasingly harsh conditions in the U.S. workplace since the 1980s, stagnant wages, the low-wage, dead-end nature of many new unskilled jobs in the service sector, and regional and industrial factors such as the ravages caused by factory relocations to the South or outside of the U.S. from rural industrial areas of the Midwest.

Krugman's methodological allegiances seemed to underwrite his own incrementalist politics and his patronizing incomprehension of the Bernie Sanders campaign's focus on changing national priorities rather than supplying detailed policy papers. As for Trump, Krugman had only scorn for the Republican businessman's ignorance of policy and government, his compulsive lying, and his campy personality; little did he suspect that part of the power of Trump's populist appeal lay in giving voice to legitimate economic grievances.

The elections also threw glaring light on a largely one-way culture of loyalty that was condescending towards the Democratic base, as expressed in the phrase "firewalls" and the slogan "I'm With Her!" An echo of 1970s feminism's politics of solidarity, the slogan seemed in 2016 to place the burden of political commitment more on voters than the candidate. Much was owed to her, or so it seemed to imply, and she owed little in return beyond the gift of her person. She had already earned our vote by virtue of who she was and her past record. That may have appealed to older liberal voters and their battle-tested loyalties, but apparently much less so to independent-minded young voters, especially women. Clinton's other slogan, "Stronger Together!", though bland, avoided these pitfalls.

Perhaps part of seventy-four-year-old Bernie Sanders's success with younger voters was due to the fact that he, unexpectedly for someone of his age cohort, made few overt claims on their loyalty; after all, he had to win them over first with his social-democratic ideas and program. His advanced age, combined with a forceful yet respectful tone and demeanor towards voters, struck many as fresh and captured the attention of many of them. As for Trump, an old-fashioned paternalist, he countered the Clinton slogans with the more vigorous, "I'm With You!" that pledged to take care of distressed voters' grievances and promised results in return for their ballots. He presented a clearer trade or, if you like, a more legible deal. Reflecting Trump's image as the ever decisive entrepreneur and problem-solver, this slogan spoke not of the past but of the future, promising change and a better life.

The Democratic Party establishment's longstanding internal culture of loyalty has had two other consequences as well: first, a willingness (shared by mainstream news media) to engage in high-handed and disrespectful treatment of insurgent candidates like Howard Dean, Barack Obama, and

Bernie Sanders who threaten their control of the Party[112]; second, in the case of Clinton, a startling devotion to dysfunctional campaign and DNC staffs at the expense of her chances of winning (the scandalous hacked emails of Huma Abedin and her estranged husband, former Congressman Anthony Weiner; Debbie Wasserman Schultz, ousted and discredited DNC Chair; Donna Brazile, former manager of Al Gore's disastrous 2000 campaign, who replaced Wasserman Schultz).

In the case of Clinton's inner circle, the one-way culture of loyalty described previously was abandoned in favor of a two-way sense of obligation, equally counterproductive. In the end, the existential threats presented by Trump's aggressive campaign, the controversy over Clinton's private email server, and the contents of the hacked emails were not taken seriously, especially those revealing active DNC collusion against the Sanders campaign, and preemptive countermeasures were not pursued.[113] The rest is history.

CHAPTER SIX

Learning from the Dynamics of Political Intimidation and Bullying

The unexpected victory of a misogynist, far-right white nationalist candidate in November 2016 convulsed the body politic and demoralized the Democratic Party. Donald Trump's successful candidacy represents the mainstreaming of the political violence that preceded his election and will persist once he has left office. In particular, the presidential campaign and its aftermath have revealed the many snares and traps that envelop any target of political intimidation and fear-mongering. So to help guide readers through this treacherous political terrain, I've distilled the essential features of the dynamics of political intimidation we've encountered in previous chapters and the dangers they present to those seeking to oppose the destructive policies of the current administration.

Preemptive Strike: Creating Public Facts on the Ground

In today's media-saturated politics, the element of **surprise** is primordial. It bespeaks power. Creating a sensation or buzz is everything. It may involve **aggressive timing** (as President-elect, in the middle of the night at 3 AM, during the State of the Union Address, during a newspaper interview, meeting privately with Putin in the presence of other foreign leaders, just as a category four hurricane is making landfall, etc.) or **unexpected locations** (a formal dinner in Germany with G-20 leaders, the annual Boy Scouts of America Scout Jamboree).

Above all, it involves **extreme content**, saying or doing the unthinkable: broadcasting racist attack ads, calling for the execution of African-American youths before the case goes to trial, vilifying newly arrived First Ladies, mocking a triple amputee's military honor, paralyzing and shutting down the federal government and then declaring it dysfunctional, publicizing names of confidential military whistleblowers, prosecuting journalists who refuse to reveal confidential sources, questioning a sitting president's nationality, bringing weapons to rallies, marching armed through a college campus chanting anti-Semitic slogans, inciting supporters at political rallies to rough up protestors, calling on the Russians to provide an opponent's missing email messages, threatening a candidate with incarceration and assassination, smearing a federal district judge overseeing a personal lawsuit in terms of his ethnicity in the hope he will overreact and thereby be forced to recuse himself from the case, encouraging law enforcement officers to physically abuse arrestees, using one's office of sheriff to terrorize entire local communities, publicly exploiting the grief of a Navy Seal widow after a botched raid, using a trigger camera from the podium to single out transgender members of the audience for harassment (Milo Yiannopolous), threatening Jews and Blacks with retaliation for fomenting violence (NRA video), harassing professors of color critical of white nationalist politics, expressing sympathy for violent white supremacist and neo-Nazi demonstrators, criminalizing the free speech of citizens who support the international academic boycott of Israeli universities in protest against Israel's occupation of Palestine and calling them anti-Semitic, etc.

It also entails **speed**, **volume**, and **reach of delivery**: mobilization of print, cable, broadcast, and social media, endless repetition, spreading talking points, launching Internet bots and armies of trolls, etc. to overwhelm adversaries. Here Trump's Twitter account plays a crucial role. It is not some quirky personality feature of an eccentric CEO; in his hands it has been transformed into a fundamental tool of power and political communication. Today Trump and his Republican allies don't mete out measured doses of political intimidation and bullying only occasionally; it is extreme, 24/7, and all the time.

Intimidation of this kind **seizes the initiative**, occupies the news cycle, and by virtue of its speed and power overpowers our capacity for reflective thought, and causes the hormonal response to well up, fight or flight? It also seizes the nervous system[114] and **creates emotional facts on the ground** (the victim's responses, but also ours and the media's) that **put the target on the defensive** and the rest of us on notice. This is the personal, psychological dimension of political bullying that Trump expertly intensifies to the highest degree through his outsized persona. Here, politics becomes personal at the expense of any consideration of the issues.

Public Bullying

Political bullying behind closed doors presents certain advantages, such as the absence of witnesses and accountability, but in the current harsh public arena of U.S. national politics with its violent gladiatorial theater of dominance the opposite is true. In **public bullying** the presence of an audience or witnesses, rather than putting a check on the aggressor party, actually enables it to malign and smear the opponent's reputation and character in terms of her, his, or a group's **nonconformity to social norms**. These are norms related to gendered and class-defined behavior, strength of character, personality type, physical appearance and self-presentation, mental soundness, social, ideological, and political affiliations, etc. In Trump's case, his public bullying relies on deploying norms against others, even as he freely breaks or rewrites them through his own actions as circumstance and opportunity warrant. Such is his apparent power and freedom as a fully entrepreneurial politician and media celebrity. As stated previously, for many of his supporters Trump's violent behavior communicates freedom and authenticity. In a sense, he is the ultimate practitioner of what political philosopher Wendy Brown has termed the declarative mode of neoconservative discourse, in which inner conviction preempts questions of veracity or facticity.[115]

In public, **extremely legible appearances** are the rule, and any ambiguity or complexity leaves one open to invidious interpretation and attack in the form of mocking, taking remarks out of context, stigmatization, ostracization, guilt by association, being ignored, etc. Sometimes the violence takes the form of recruitment, otherwise known as hazing, of a submissive target into a group of sovereign subjects (for example, the fraternity of the power-brokers), but in political campaigns exclusion and defeat of the adversary are generally the goal. The **manipulation of appearances** by the assailant is his or her most powerful tool. The target suffers not only an isolating and humiliating attack but—second humiliation—boxed in by the overwhelmingly *public* (witnessed and recorded) nature of the act, has no choice but to respond.

In this scenario the victim's reputation, body, and speech are all purposely violated. And this multiple violation is already read as the **forced public revelation of a weakness** in the victim previously unknown to the public (and perhaps even to the target); or more accurately, as **a sign of *potential*, if not actual, weakness,** one that may not manifest itself now but *could* at any time. It thus becomes the subject of endless speculation by others and the media. You remain tainted: what political philosopher Brian Massumi calls in another context an "affective pariah."[116] Moreover, if you respond or protest, it dignifies the accusation and simply confirms the adversary's power and dominance, and you risk remaining prisoner of his or her smear or misrepresentation (a danger often cited by reluctant Democratic politicians).

But that is not all: if you so much as name the smear, the perpetrator can turn the tables on you, accuse *you* of being the aggressor, and then claim victimhood for him or herself. This is especially the case when attacks take the passive-aggressive form of rumormongering or repeating hearsay or of a "joke" that disavows any responsibility for the slander, leaving it up to the victim to name it as such. Bullied, one loses the right of response; the slightest reaction elicits another assault: "Are you being hostile?" Here, the aggressor enjoys all control and escapes any accountability, especially in the national arena of politics if the bully is white and male. Such is his privilege. On the other hand, in keeping publicly silent you risk either appearing complicit with the charge or confirming your own vulnerability and making yourself dependent on the sympathy and goodwill of bystanders and voters to protect you. This has been Democrats' strategy of choice for years.

But of course the public is fickle, and the violence of the assault deepens the impression of one's own vulnerability. And in the public political theater of dominance vulnerability denotes weakness, a flaw fatal to most candidates. **There is no supreme witness or arbiter to which you can appeal for justice.** That god is dead. So **you are on your own**—or least made to feel that way. Michael Dukakis, John Kerry, Barack Obama, and even the more combative Hillary Clinton learned this to their sorrow. Political animal that he is, Bill Clinton was a better fighter, but only when Newt Gingrich put him on the ropes; only then did he develop a rapid response team that countered outlandish Republican allegations within the same news cycle with some success.

The Politics of Destruction

Preemptive attacks are a game of pure power; they are all the more terrifying in that they appear *unmotivated* by virtue of being so unexpected. In the current Republican onslaught, it is crucial to remember that such attacks are *without any apparent meaning* other than conserving their power and advantage, destabilizing and defeating opponents, and destroying the legacy of the New Deal. They seem to value creative destruction even over privatization. At their most extreme, in the hands of the Republicans in Washington these assaults are profoundly nihilistic—heedless of any social, ethical, or psychological boundaries.

Arbitrary and chaotic, our new masters attack the weak and the strong, the fearful and the indifferent alike, throwing opponents off guard while projecting an aura of impunity and displaying no conscience. As we said earlier, their aggression strives to impress upon both actual and potential victims its literally *boundless* character that surpasses their most dire fears. They stand beyond any appeal and are unreachable except perhaps through fear and their sense of self-preservation.

Before the 2016 elections, this may have looked like empty macho bluster (however, see Chapter One), but since January 20, 2017 their appointments, executive orders, and budget proposal actions have spoken. At times they seem to do what they do merely *because they can.* Here, power is its own justification. In the rush to destroy the federal government as we know it, it now appears that the Republicans are following no positive electoral rationale, at least in the short term. The proposed budget cuts don't even spare their base, who are in for a rough course of political reeducation about what they can expect from government. It looks like political suicide, or more frighteningly, an act of murder-suicide.[117]

Their long game is counterrevolution; they are bent on recasting citizens' relationship to government and state services, but in the near term they seem bent on bringing the Dawn of Destruction and Last Things. Violent political Rapture that terrifies but—like Trump—may also fascinate some voters. This is where the swaggering street punk and the violent patrician/aristocrat who is indifferent to death and to the fate of others meet up and shape-shift together with free-market fundamentalists and fanatics.

With an abusive CEO like Trump, the endless dynamics of bullying that seem to invade all aspects of politics have come to match the limitless nature of unregulated capitalism itself that will monetize anything, exchange anything, buy anything, exploit anything.[118] In Trump's new political world, as in unfettered markets, everything is fair game. This is what both the resistance and the Democratic Party must understand and anticipate.

Many of Trump's assaults have been expected reactions to challenges by journalists and political adversaries, but, as we've seen, they can still shock and surprise by what they denigrate or target: once again, Barack Obama's nationality,

Fox News reporter Megyn Kelly's physiology. *New York Times* journalist Serge Kovaleski's disability. Khizr and Gazala Kahn's religion. U.S. District Judge Gonzalo Curiel's ethnicity. Mika Brzezinski's IQ. Or Hillary Clinton's physical safety. As we've said before, Trump practices a negative identity politics of degraded subjecthood that relentlessly seeks to dishonor and defame all comers.

It is especially effective against political rivals like the Democrats, who seem to invest as much in their *identity* as in political action. An attacker like Trump seeks to besmirch that self-image. He knows full well that for the victim to respond would not only dignify both the attack and the attacker but also undermine the victim's public reputation. In the cheap cynical script that dominates U.S. public life, both the target and the attacker are held equally to blame, an attitude that almost always favors the assailant, who most often couldn't care less about his or her reputation, so long as he or she emerges as the most powerful party. Power is its own positive PR. Finally, it is not simply a single act of aggression, but rather one that is repeatable, but unpredictably so. When successful, the act of intimidation instills a new timeline of perpetual threat through injecting fear of a dreaded fate and ungraspable future into the present. This is political virtuality at its most potent.

Now that Republicans control both the White House and Congress, they have moved from verbal and physical threats to actual fear-inducing decisions: imposing travel bans, rescinding the Deferred Action for Childhood Arrivals (DACA) program and preparing to deport millions of other undocumented immigrants, lifting corporate oversight and sanctions, imposing embargoes on federal agencies and their data, authorizing dumping of mining industry chemicals into rivers and streams, resuming oil drilling in the Arctic, opening up national parks to logging and fracking, banning transgender recruits from the military, accepting the resignation of all U.S. Attorneys, stripping people of Medicaid coverage, crippling the EPA, cutting Health and Human Services by 13%, cutting Pell Grants, reducing National

Institute of Health and National Ocean and Atmosphere Administration budgets by 18%, etc.

Many of these policies don't require explicit congressional legislation but simply executive action. Arguably the most consequential act of political intimidation, exploiting our collective hopes and fears and targeting the entire planet, was the announcement in June 2017 by the White House of the U.S.'s withdrawal from the Paris climate agreement. The timing and manner of doing the unthinkable couldn't have been worse—or more cruelly exquisite. Trump acted as the supreme agent of lawless national sovereignty and global dread. The future is here, and it is a waking nightmare.

Snares and Traps: Denial

If recent actions since November 2016 have anything to suggest, it is that Democratic leaders conduct themselves as if they are not interested in taking the full measure of the destructive methods of their opponents, or worse, as if they are looking for reasons *not* to take political violence seriously, perhaps in the hope that it will cease or go away, much in the way of an abused partner or spouse who pleads, "Oh, honey, you really didn't mean it, did you?" But of course "honey" did mean it, or rather, sees no reason to stop and can't help himself or herself (philandering, drinking, physical violence, verbal abuse, psychological harassment, etc.) and will do it again. And again. One of the goals of the massive January 21st Women's March was to disabuse party leaders of that illusion.

Still, like the hapless Republican establishment during the primaries and the Clinton campaign in the general election, many liberal and progressive Democrats and sympathetic media pundits continue to embrace a consoling fiction, in the way that victims of bullies often do, namely, that Trump is an insecure narcissist (thanks to his father), a phony (failed businessman, in debt, etc.), ignorant (of the art of government and foreign policy), a liar (delusional), and self-destructive (reckless and unethical dealmaker) and *therefore* bound to meet his political end soon.

All of which could turn out to be true, but it overlooks how it is that Trump even got this far and, more important, why Trump's supposed weaknesses or character flaws may end up being irrelevant in light of the success with which Trump and the Republican leadership, still behind him, implement their extremist agenda of defunding public services and destroying federal agencies and departments. Trump may be a weak and flawed human being but he, his followers, and GOP allies remain a potent political force to this day.[119]

But within the Democratic establishment, old tribal loyalties and discredited strategies remain strong. In the midst of this political emergency, what did the Democratic Party establishment first devote its energies to? Electing Tom Perez as chair of the Democratic National Committee. A liberal Democrat with no experience in campaigning or elected office, his candidacy was promoted by Obama to counter Keith Ellison, a politically savvy and energetic Minnesota Congressman and former Bernie Sanders supporter, who received the support of New York Senator Chuck Schumer, New York City Mayor Bill de Blasio, and nearly half of the members of the DNC but was denigrated by other party officials for his Muslim religious affiliation.

Perez's first public pronouncement was to express worry about an imminent stock market "correction," surely the top preoccupation of the Democratic base. He then proceeded to assemble a twenty-nine-member advisory committee, of which only two supported Ellison in the close race and one supported Bernie Sanders in the primaries.[120] It is true that after assuming office he went on a national tour of progressive audiences with Bernie Sanders in April 2017, but he stuck to the bland DNC script of "coming together" left over from the Clinton campaign and carefully refused to criticize the actions of Wall Street bankers or discuss the failed Democratic electoral strategies. Only thanks to the unremitting pressure exerted by activists such as the members of Indivisible, Swing Left, and other groups has the Democratic congressional leadership stood up effectively against the GOP agenda.

Snares and Traps: Blind Revenge

Political resistance to Trump should make use of all available means at its disposal, but the obsessive focus on allegations of possible Russian interference in the elections is not encouraging, because it doesn't deal with the increasing use of political violence, public bullying, and their corrosive effects. Moreover, it may seem like the vigorous response of a defeated party to an unprecedented act of political skullduggery, but it is arguably the opposite. The Trump campaign may have received and even sought Russian assistance in the form of hacked DNC emails and these charges must be investigated. But what is worrisome is the *manner* in which the Democratic establishment and media outlets have drawn conclusions based on circumstantial evidence, anonymous sources, and assurances of the intelligence agencies; have spoken freely of "treason"; and have announced "definitive" incriminating findings on a weekly basis.

This bespeaks a weakened, desperate party flailing about in search of an easy exculpating explanation for its debacle and strangely eager to trust the NSA, the CIA, and the FBI, historically no friends of democratic liberties, to protect it from Trump and his machinations. In terms of our analysis of political intimidation and bullying, this amounts to switching from one source of abuse to another and is reminiscent of nineteenth-century Sicilian local elites calling in the Mafia to protect them from roving bandits and landless peasants.

Just as startling is the willingness on the part of some Democratic leaders, operatives, and media allies to extend allegations of colluding with the Russian government to Bernie Sanders, Jill Stein, journalists who question the evidence for the allegations of Russian meddling, and Edward Snowden, who revealed massive NRA surveillance of citizens. It is almost as if they think that abusing those to their political left will restore the Democratic establishment's and mainstream media's sense of self and purpose lost last November.[121] However, it would not be the first time, nor would it be most likely the last [122] Liberal Democrats have a long history, going back to the Cold War, of red-baiting progressives in order to secure political advantage within the party and without, a history that peaked at the height of protests against the vast escalation of the Vietnam War by Lyndon Johnson, a Democrat.[123]

So even if the allegations are borne out by the ongoing FBI investigation, it may not achieve the desired political outcome of removing Trump from office. Never has Congress formally convicted a sitting U.S. president, and, in the case of the existing Republican majorities, it would destroy the GOP for the foreseeable future were they to do so.

Moreover, it would also come at the cost of rehabilitating, not only the national security and law enforcement agencies who have been engaging in unprecedented massive electronic surveillance of the U.S. population and who *themselves* meddled in the last election, but also the Democratic Party establishment, who will see no reason to rethink their failed electoral strategies and internal party culture. Like the Clinton campaign itself, it continues to focus its energies on Trump the man to the detriment of focusing on the issues and shifting our national priorities. At best, the multiple investigations reported by the media may paralyze Trump and the Republicans' national agenda; at worst they will exhaust the limited political energy and resources needed to sustain political struggle over the long haul.

Snares and Traps: Nostalgia for the Theater of Moral Shaming

Now any meaningful discussion of the dynamics of contemporary political intimidation and bullying and effective responses to them has to take into consideration the context of the public media sphere, where so much of this is played out. Long gone is old broadcast television, whose relatively unified single national audience, historically-minded readers may recall, witnessed the high moral theater of political accountability that put an end to Joseph McCarthy's anti-communist smear campaigns in 1954 during the Army-McCarthy Senate hearings. The televised proceedings climaxed when the Army's lawyer Joe Welch countered McCarthy's invidious questioning of a member of the armed services about his youthful political affiliations with the simple, shaming question, "Have you no sense of decency, sir, at long last?" The exchange initiated McCarthy's political decline.[124]

The public discrediting of a violent politician is hard to imagine today in the very fractured media landscape broken up by cable TV, AM radio, Internet streaming, and social media where decency is a scarce commodity. There are many independent publics, some quite segregated from one another. And presumably many polities, equally segregated: after all, newly elected Trump declined to issue the traditional statement that he was the president of all Americans. The rational, deliberative exchanges presumably characteristic of the old public sphere no longer exist (if they ever did fully) and have been replaced by the counterfactual and felt politics of fear in which moral shaming of violent perpetrators no longer works, but public dishonoring and disrespecting of their victims still do.

Let's be clear. The public outcry across the political spectrum against Trump's extraordinary expression of open sympathy for armed white supremacists and neo-Nazis in Charlottesville, Virginia in August 2017 should not be taken as the beginning of a revival of the old moral public sphere, but rather as the extreme exception that proves the rule.[125] Should Trump choose to resign in the near future, the culture of intimidation he embodies and has mainstreamed will remain in place furthering and protecting his and the Republican's far-right agendas. Their long game will continue.

Snares and Traps: Media Frenzies

Finally, related to the limits of the public theater of moral shaming is relying on media outlets to perform the work of political messaging and reaching concerned voters as a way to oppose the Republican agenda and its bullying tactics. It is even more fraught with hazards than depending on a telegenic politician to sustain a political movement and renew a political party in the absence of a real infrastructure. A recently published retrospective assessment by two members of Bernie Sanders's political team is highly critical of the decision they themselves made during the primaries to spend $90 million in political ads instead of investing these resources in local, face-to-face efforts.[126]

Perhaps even more to the point is the fact that although the media may constitute the "Fourth Estate," charged with holding public officials and the powerful accountable, fundamentally they are commercial enterprises for whom the bottom line, in the form of advertising revenues and viewer ratings, comes first, public service second. Like preemptive acts of political intimidation, their natural tendency is to create a buzz, which they do by sensationalizing news, engaging in speculative reporting, and employing endless repetition. They will build up a story or a reputation and then are more than happy to tear it down, as long as they can make money along the way in either direction. They have no compunction about aggressively bullying their way to profits at the expense of the public good.

The career of Jeff Zucker, former president and CEO of NBC Universal and current president of CNN, is a prime example of this strategy. He helped create Trump's reality TV show *The Apprentice* for NBC, which was instrumental in establishing Trump as a global brand and folk hero. Zucker made his company millions in promoting it. Then later at CNN, during the 2016 Republican primaries, Zucker lavished uncritical coverage of Trump's provocative speeches, rallies, and tweets while relentlessly pursuing stories about Clinton's private email server, the Clinton Foundation, and the Benghazi incident.

As for the Sanders campaign, it received some attention as a quirky, disruptive outlier, but the cable networks, including liberal MSNBC, freely ignored and sometimes mocked Sanders, even as he attracted some of the largest turnouts at his political rallies and was shifting the national conversation to the subject of extreme economic disparities; worse, the media did not hesitate to black out some of his most consequential speeches like the one he gave after pulling a historic upset victory over Clinton in the Michigan primary, which pollsters predicted she would win by twenty points.

Only after Trump became the favorite to win the nomination did CNN and other networks begin to turn a critical eye on his campaign, but they veered to the opposite extreme. They were equally aggressive and sensationalizing with otherwise legitimate stories and arguably created a backlash among undecided voters that favored Trump as Election Day approached. [127] Mediaquant calculated that Trump received $5.8 billion in free media, $2.9 billion more than Hillary Clinton.[128] Ever since, the news media have had a field day, as Trump wrested control of the 24/7 news cycle, but in return, with every tweet he made them the gift of an attention-getting headline and potential scoop. Although Trump now openly views the "media" as his enemies, they remain his secret collaborators, for he and they both benefit from the relationship. As CBS Chairman Les Moonves admitted during the primaries regarding their coverage of Trump, "It may not be good for America, but it is damn good for CBS."

In the end there is no reason to think that the media are our allies. The Women's March, the congressional town hall confrontations, and the flooding of airports with protestors opposing the Muslim travel ban took advantage of the media's need for headline news, but they did not remain their prisoner. The media's handling of the Russian email hacking and money laundering scandals won't be any different in terms of overkill of an otherwise important story.

Media frenzies in a harsh political environment have their own rhythms, and they aren't necessarily those of progressive political movements. Like bona fide political bullies, with their cheap cynicism ever on the lookout for speculative hearsay, false equivalences, a newsworthy misstatement, ambiguous motive, or character flaw, they will empty any issue of its substance. The media are probably more than happy to see Trump impeached, but they can't be counted on to publicize and educate citizens in the substance of issues that they care about and will continue to care about after Trump has departed.

CONCLUSION

Renewing Politics

> We believe that the next four years depend on Americans across the country standing indivisible against the Trump agenda. We believe that buying into false promises or accepting partial concessions will only further empower Trump to victimize us and our neighbors.
>
> *Indivisible: A Practical Guide for Resisting the Trump Agenda*

> I accept that aggression is part of life and hence part of politics as well. But aggression can and must be separated from violence (violence being one form that aggression assumes), and there are ways of giving form to aggression in the service of democratic life, including "antagonism" and discursive conflict, strikes, civil disobedience, and even revolution.
>
> Judith Butler, *Frames of War*[129]

On Our Own

Unprecedented acts of political intimidation and public bullying demand an equally unprecedented response. This is not a fearful reaction but rather—as I hope the preceding pages have made clear—a necessary and level-headed conclusion. There is nothing we should expect in the way of understanding, hearing, collaboration, or exchange of views from the Trump administration or the Republican leadership that will slow down or stop the far-right juggernaut. [130]

We are on our own. This has its advantages in terms of strategy and tactics that avoid some of the illusions of the past, like the hopeful expectation of bipartisanship in dealing with far-right extremists. Thus it is important to understand that Bernie Sander's public offer to work with the Republicans on various issues is no fool's bid for collaboration across the aisle. Instead, he is hastening the day when the Trump administration's sham populism fails, as it may do with his cabinet appointments of business executives and billionaires, who made their fortunes by causing direct harm to others and his proposals to cut healthcare insurance and Medicaid. That was the purpose of town halls Sanders began hosting with Trump voters in February 2017 now that the Trump-Republican agenda threatened to become public policy.

The Trump-led 24/7 counterrevolution is upon us and is re-writing the political script as we speak, taking full advantage of social media to bypass party establishments and mainstream news media and deploying all the means the federal government has now placed at its disposal to intimidate opponents and pursue its far-right agenda. Throughout this short book, I've made few allusions to historical precedents of authoritarian regimes coming to power, especially in Europe, and fascism is a word I rarely use. But we live in politically fluid times and the political field is still wide open.

As I said previously, Trump has indulged in a pre-fascist political style that is aggrieved, xenophobic, nostalgic, paranoid, and physically violent. It curries the support of white supremacists and the Internet-based alt. right. It traffics in counterfactual felt politics and outlandish accusations. It enjoys a mass following and indicts the basic institutions of liberal democratic societies: political parties, free press, the judiciary, the electoral process, the law and its routine protections. However, the harsh healthcare bills have proven to be unpopular even among Republican governors, and some of his more ardent followers have softened their support.[131] He may have missed the opportunity to exploit the political opening created by his violent campaign's surprise victory.

As Robert O. Paxton, a leading historian of fascism, remarked, to maintain mobilization of their followers political leaders like Trump must expand relentlessly and seek new opportunities to affirm and secure their power (new enemies, threats, crises).[132] Should Trump and congressional Republicans find themselves stymied by our fierce opposition, the steady drip of leaks from the intelligence agencies that are slowly neutralizing key players in the White House (first Michael Flynn, then son-in-law Jared, and now Donald, Jr.), the opposition of foreign leaders, or simply by the daily routine of Beltway politics, the inertias of governing, and Republicans' miscalculations, they may take yet more extreme measures to maintain their momentum that circumvent laws and the Constitution: firing Special Counsel Robert Mueller investigating Russian meddling in the election and Attorney General Jeff Sessions and issuing presidential pardons, on the one hand, or manufacturing international crises, starting a new war, unleashing domestic political provocateurs, or declaring a state of emergency in the wake of another terrorist attack, on the other.

Trump's statements regarding the North Korean nuclear threat and his expressions of sympathy for white supremacists and neo-Nazis can be read as possible signs of this. Since Trump has made political intimidation the very content of both his campaign and administration, the temptation would be for him even to substitute violent actions for substantive policy achievements pure and simple.

In any event, as I've argued throughout this book, his legacy will necessarily include the mainstreaming of political intimidation and public bullying and a misogynist, white nationalist agenda that will outlast whatever policies he and his Republican allies implement and will affect electoral politics for years to come. Moreover, even after Trump is gone, the chances are high that specter of another defiant and authoritarian white "savior" CEO, not from discredited Wall Street but most likely from Silicon Valley, will haunt the land.

Rewriting the Political Script

However, Trump, the radicalized GOP leadership, and the Tea Party Republicans aren't the only ones recasting how we do politics. Four years ago Occupy Wall Street, with its encampments and novel organizing methods, refocused political debate on unprecedented class and wealth disparities and the politics of redistribution. [133] "The 1%" became a powerful slogan, and Bernie Sanders made it his own, upending the Democratic Party in the primaries.

If any lessons are to be drawn from the recent history of right-wing political intimidation and lackluster Democratic response, they surely entail, to echo Sanders, a political revolution within the Democratic Party itself in terms of identity, self-image, self-governance, programs, political messaging, fundraising, forms of mobilization of the liberal and progressive base, and appeals to distressed voters.

The goal is to break out of the institutional capture the Democratic Party underwent with the financialization of the U.S. economy, and the domination by the banking sector that turned it away from working- and middle-class voters and handed it over to big corporate donors. But there will be no successful party politics without the direct pressure of street politics, and no successful street politics without some form of political representation and devotion to the nuts and bolts of governing. And both are necessary to undo the current public climate of fear and intimidation. The two go together, but never easily.

Sanders's original insight is that involvement in politics at the local level and repopulating minor offices with progressives bring street and party politics closer together. It is a crucial way to build a new political infrastructure independent of national party politics and to maintain street mobilization over the long haul. Our attention span is short but this is a long-term project. In particular this approach has the advantage of freeing the political process from the militaristic agendas and free-market dogmas that dominate national debates and block progressive policies at the federal level. It also frees the political process from the presidential elections that make political achievement depend on a single electoral outcome or candidate; this is why they are often disappointing and demobilizing and feed the already deep well of disaffection and cynicism among voters.

Locally, what matters more is tackling issues of immediate concern to voters and making sure government works for them. At the same time, what is also needed are a new mobilizing program and narrative that unite progressives and liberals to counter the far right's agenda and its destructive cult of unregulated markets, savage entrepreneurship, and small government. For without a narrative about the future in place, if and when Trump's sham populism fails, many disappointed voters will be tempted to lapse back into an attitude of protective cynicism that blames all political factions equally and disengages from politics altogether, or worse, they will follow the right's lead in blaming entire communities for the broken promises. Dismantling the current culture of political intimidation and fear-mongering will be no simple task.

In the end, the impetus must come from a mobilized citizenry, without which the Democratic Party will continue to be the private quasi-monopoly of access to political power and public office and the ineffective force it is today. In fact, the fierce public reaction against dismantling Obamacare, led by Indivisible, Swing Left, and other groups building on the progressive populism of Bernie Sanders' campaign, is a hopeful sign that public perceptions concerning the role of the state in ensuring individual and general welfare may be moving away from the radical individualism that so marks our public life.[134]

Unlike the Democratic Party establishment, we can't forget that the Republicans are cruel, remorseless adversaries, who play for keeps. There is no pleasing or appeasing them. At this juncture anything is possible in the way of political bullying and intimidation: more cruel legislation, impugning opponents' motives, smearing resisters with fake allegations, physical threats to entire communities, dirty tricks, and defunding cherished civil society institutions. It is important to call these acts for what they are: *forms of political violence.*

The real revolution will be among citizens themselves. And it is already underway: protestors opposing the Muslim travel ban flooded U.S. Customs at airports, the Women's

March in January brought out three million people, Black Lives Matter and Our Revolution (created by former Sanders organizers) have forged an activist alliance, and Swing Left and the 6,000 local chapters of Indivisible are actively pressuring politicians to resist Trump's political intimidation and acts of government. The outpouring of angry citizens at congressional town halls has given Republican congressional representatives pause and slowed down the march to repeal the Affordable Care Act. For once, our side, breaking free of the endless intimidation, took the initiative and enjoyed the intimidating element of surprise. And so we created our own affective or emotional "facts on the ground."

We may be on our own but we are not alone. In resisting together we are forced to step outside of ourselves. It is about getting things done as much as affirming an identity. As Sanders concluded his public interview with *Democracy Now!* host Amy Goodman and disappointed voters shortly after the election, "Remember, it's not about you. It's about the future of this planet. It's about your kids and your grandchildren, it is about American democracy, it is about some very fundamental issues."[135]

About the Author

Roddey Reid is Professor Emeritus, University of California, San Diego, where he taught classes on the modern cultures and societies of the U.S., France, and Japan. He is the author of *Families in Jeopardy: Regulating the Social Body in France, 1750-1910*; co-editor of *Doing Science + Culture*; and author of *Globalizing Tobacco Control: Anti-Smoking Campaigns in California, France, and Japan*. His latest writing has been on trauma, daily life, and the culture of intimidation and bullying in the U.S. and Europe. He hosts a personal blog called "UnSafe Thoughts" on bullying and the fluidity of politics in dangerous times. He is a member of Indivisible San Francisco.

NOTES

[1] Michel Foucault, "On the Genealogy of Ethics: An Overview of Work in Progress." Afterword, in Hubert L. Dreyfus and Paul Rabinow, *Michel Foucault: Beyond Structuralism and Hermeneutics*, 2nd ed. (Chicago, 1983), 231-32; Senator Elizabeth Warren, Joyous Persistence Event, San Francisco, 1 June 2017 https://www.youtube.com/watch?v=-CAKV1ZwoeM. Accessed 15 July 2017.

[2] Brian Massumi, *The Politics of Everyday Fear* (Minnesota, 1993), ix.

[3] For a consideration of how contemporary political intimidation and public bullying are not only a political and emotional challenge but also a conceptual challenge to ingrained habits of analysis and thought, especially in the social sciences, see my review essay on Charles Derber and Yale Magrass's book, *Bully Nation*: "*Bully Nation* and Our Current Predicament," *Contemporary Sociology* 46.3 (May 2017): 273-76.

[4] Trump practices what sociologist Isaac Martin calls "a rhetorical posture of defiance in the face of class condescension" of economic and social elites. It is a posture he terms "vicarious populism," whose rudeness when practiced by a wealthy man like Trump and many of his middle-class followers earns them membership--in their eyes at least--in the common people. For his skeptical appraisal of recent studies that view Trump voters as primarily poor and working-class whites, see Isaac Martin, "Deplorable Yourself," *Books and Ideas*, 7 Nov. 2016. http://www.booksandideas.net/Deplorable-yourself.html. Accessed 30 Aug. 2017.

5 Quoted by Sanjay Chaturvedi and Timothy Doyle, *Climate Terror: A Critical Geopolitics of Climate Change* (Palgrave Macmillan, 2105), 7.

6 In U.S. parlance, political "liberals" traditionally subscribe to the social and legal protections afforded by government established during the New Deal in the 1930s and 40s and expanded during the 1960s and 70s; they also defend civil liberties against the intrusions of federal, state, and local government. In other national contexts they would be called mainstream or centrist social-democrats.

7 Wayne Barrett, Foreword, *Trump: The Greatest Show on Earth*, Kindle revised edition (Regan Arts, 2016). The 2016 foreword is only available in the Kindle e-book edition.

8 Privatization and authoritarian rule make perfect bedfellows, for, as political philosopher Elizabeth Anderson reminds us, the modern firm is by nature a form of authoritarian government (and I would add, in that regard, not unlike family businesses generally); see her *Private Government: How Employers Rule Our Lives (and Why We Don't Talk about It)* (Princeton, 2017).

9 For the disjunctive theory of presidential transitions when the governing party is caught between old and new political paradigms, see, for example, Corey Robin, "The Politics Trump Makes: Is Trump, Like Carter, a Disjunctive President?" *n+1*, 11 Jan. 2017. https://nplusonemag.com/online-only/online-only/the-politics-trump-makes/. Accessed 20 Jan. 2017. For free-market ideologues' longstanding goal of having citizens and residents view themselves primarily as human capital and consumers and transforming their relation to government, see Wendy Brown, *Undoing the Demos: Neoliberalism's Stealth Revolution* (Zone Books, 2015), 35-41.

10 Tom McCarthy, "The Promise: Trump Supporters Still Fixate on Clinton as Mood Darkens," *The Guardian* 20 July 2017. https://www.theguardian.com/us-news/2017/jul/20/donald-trump-support-base-hillary-

clinton-hatred-pennsylvania?utm_source=esp&utm_medium=Email&utm_c ampaign=GU+Today+USA++Collections+2017&utm_term=2 35837&subid=22086658&CMP=GT_US_collection. Accessed 20 July 2017.

[11] Naomi Klein, *No Is Not Enough: Resisting Trump's Shock Politics and Winning the World We Need* (Haymarket Books, 2017).

[12] Trump's consorting with the violent politics of extreme right-wing groups—including the newer Internet-based alt.right--is hardly unique among U.S. politicians. It was common practice by conservatives throughout the twentieth century. Trump is simply more open about his sympathies. See historian of U.S. conservatism Rick Pearlstein, "I Thought I Understood the American Right. Trump Proved Me Wrong," *New York Times Magazine* 11 April 2017. https://www.nytimes.com/2017/04/11/magazine/i-thought-i-understood-the-american-right-trump-proved-me-wrong.html?smid=fb-share&_r=0. Accessed 30 April 2017.

[13] Klein, *No Is Not Enough*, 19.

[14] Even the attendees of the annual convention of the Conservative Political Action Conference, a very establishment organization, enthusiastically acclaimed Trump's February 24, 2017 incendiary speech denouncing the media and corporate elites: Glenn Thrush, "Trump's Blistering Speech at CPAC Follows Bannon's Blueprint," *New York Times*, 24 Feb. 2017. https://www.nytimes.com/2017/02/24/us/politics/trump-conservative-political-action-conference-speech.html?_r=0. Accessed 28 Feb. 2017. As of March 7, 2017 95% of Republicans approved Trump's job performance. And after the February speech, the percentage of Republicans who trust Trump and not the media as their news source went up from 78% to 86% according to the Quinnipiac University Poll: https://poll.qu.edu/national/release-detail?ReleaseID=2436. Accessed 7 March 2017. However, dismantling the Affordable

Care Act and Medicaid is another matter: by March 22 subsequent to the release of the Trump/Republican health care proposal to cut Medicaid benefits, Trump's support among Republicans dropped 14 points to 81%. https://poll.qu.edu/national/release-detail?ReleaseID=2442. Accessed 22 March 2017.

However, it has remained stable throughout the ensuing turmoil of his administration: as of May 24 his support among Republicans was 84% even as support for the second healthcare bill received the support of only 42% of Republicans polled but (dropping later to 37% in a June 28 poll while his approval rating among the GOP remained steady even as the proportion of those who strongly approved weakened); see https://poll.qu.edu/national/release-detail?ReleaseID=2460. Accessed 25 May and 17 July 2017; Nate Silver, "Donald Trump's Base is Shrinking," *FiveThirtyEight*, 24 May 2017. https://fivethirtyeight.com/features/donald-trumps-base-is-shrinking/. Accessed 17 July 2017. After Trump's statements concerning white supremacist and neo-Nazi demonstrators in Charlottesville, he still enjoyed a 77% approval rating among Republicans according to the August 23, 2017 Quinnipiac University Poll. https://poll.qu.edu/national/release-detail?ReleaseID=2482. Accessed 26 August 2017.

15 Brown, *Undoing the Demos*, 38-45, 122-31. For more on specific transformations of the workplace by new corporate management practices and the political implications of the rise of the tyrannical boss in the 1980s, see Chapter Two. To be clear, even absent the contemporary promotion of the autocratic boss, the private sector would not be a mainstay of democratic culture for the simple reason that it never has been. As former corporate attorney and federal government lawyer Christopher Brown writes, "CEOs rule over private realms where speech is not free, and the ideas of their subjects are the property of the sovereign. Their control over the things employees say and do extends outside the office, and even after the end of employment"; Christopher Brown, "You're

Fired: Democracy, Dystopia and the Cult of the CEO," *Shift Newco*, 15 March 2017. https://shift.newco.co/youre-fired-democracy-dystopia-and-the-cult-of-the-ceo-83a3a9b24531#.labya7uxj. Accessed 20 March 2017. For an important discussion of the authoritarian nature of the modern firm, but with no reference to the managerial and financial revolution in the 1980s, see Anderson, *Private Government*.

[16] Patricia Baird Windle and Eleanor J. Bader, *Targets of Hatred: Anti-Abortion Terrorism* (Palgrave, 2001); Loic Wacquant, *Prisons of Poverty* (Minnesota, 2009); Michelle Alexander, *The New Jim Crow: Mass Incarceration in the Age of Color-Blindness* (New Press, 2010), 12-14; David Gordon, *Fat and Mean: The Corporate Squeeze of Working Americans and the Myth of Managerial "Downsizing,"* (Free Press, 1996); Joel H. Neuman and Robert A. Baron, "Workplace Violence and Workplace Aggression: Evidence Concerning Specific Forms, Potential Causes, and Preferred Targets," *Journal of Management* 24.3 (1998): 391-409. The prison system was not long in undergoing privatization in turn, followed by the logistical and security operations of the U.S. military with the advent of the Iraq War.

[17] During the 1990s astonished citizens watched as national political life seemed to spin slowly out of control. This unsettling spectacle was fueled early on by the specter of unchecked government and citizen-sponsored armed violence that raised its head far from the nation's capital, in Waco, Texas. There a drama unfolded that would result in the largest terrorist bombing on American soil in the twentieth century: in April 1993 the FBI attacked the Branch Davidian cult's compound with gas grenades and armored personnel carriers, and the ensuing fires wiped out all the residents. Two years later, in 1995, white supremacists Timothy McVeigh and Terry Nichols retaliated by blowing up the Federal Building in Oklahoma City, Oklahoma, killing 168 people.

[18] Douglas Kellner, *Grand Theft: Media Spectacle and a Stolen Election* (Rowman & Littleton, 2001). On Democrats'

minds were surely memories of recent Republican "October Surprises," which in the eyes of many voters handed them two other presidential victories: in 1968 when Henry Kissinger working for Richard Nixon's presidential campaign sabotaged the Paris Peace Accords, which were set to announce an agreement in Vietnam on the eve of the election and effectively guaranteed Democratic Hubert Humphrey's defeat; and in 1980 when Republicans reportedly convinced the Iranian government not to release American embassy employees taken hostage during the Iranian Revolution until after the election thus helping secure Ronald Reagan's victory. The recent release of confidential documents has confirmed Democrats' long-held suspicions regarding Kissinger and Nixon's skullduggery: James Farrell, "Nixon's Vietnam Treachery," *New York Times*, 31 Dec. 2016. https://www.nytimes.com/2016/12/31/opinion/sunday/nixons-vietnam-treachery.html?_r=0. Accessed 17 July 2017. The allegations concerning the return of American hostages remain a subject of dispute.

19 Brian Massumi, "The Future Birth of The Affective Fact: The Political Ontology of Threat" in *Ontopower: War, Powers, and the State of Exception* (Duke, 2015), 189-205; Mick Taussig. "Terror as Usual: Walter Benjamin's Theory of History as a State of Siege," *Social Text* 23 (Autumn/Winter 1989): 20.

20 However, it must be noted that the suspension of the constitutional protections of due process, probable cause, and safeguards against cruel and unusual punishment in the current state of exception dating from September 2001 was long in the making. Crucial to this process were the quite legal state disciplinary measures in immigration and domestic incarceration such as the designation of prisoners as gang members and their subsequent indefinite detention in solitary confinement in "supermax" prisons.

This inhumane treatment of prisoners has been exempt from judicial review. Colin Dayan has termed the cumulative effect of these measures the "radical substitution of penal for civil life." See Colin Dayan, "Due Process and Legal Confinement," *South Atlantic Quarterly* 107.3 (July 2008): 485-507. See also Judith Butler, *Precarious Life: The Powers of Mourning and Violence* (Verso, 2004), 50-100; David Matlin, *Prison inside the New America: From Vernooykill Creek to Abu Ghraib*, 2nd ed. (North Atlantic Books, 2007); Nasser Hussain, "Beyond Norm and Exception: Guantánamo." *Critical Inquiry* 33 (Summer 2007): 734-53. The domestic supermax penitentiaries were one of the models for the prisons at Abu Ghraib and Guantánamo Bay.

21 Two of the most notorious examples of intimidation of U.S. citizens related to the Iraq War that exposed their targets to possible death were first, the public outing in the news media of CIA covert officer Valerie Plame by Vice President Dick Cheney's office in retaliation against her husband ambassador Joseph Wilson's publication of his doubts concerning the Bush Administration's claims that Saddam Hussein possessed weapons of mass destruction.

Second was Defense Secretary Donald Rumsfeld's revelation of the confidential identity of the U.S. Army soldier, who, at great personal risk to himself, had forwarded to military officials the infamous trove of photographs documenting the abuse, torture, and rape of Iraqi detainees in Abu Ghraib prison. In both cases, the goal was to silence other potential critics and whistleblowers within and without the government and the armed services. Equally pernicious was the prosecution of journalists like *New York Times* reporter James Risen, who refused to reveal the identity of confidential sources related to the whistleblowing of abusive military and surveillance practices. The Obama administration continued and expanded the pursuit of journalists.

22 Douglas Jehl and David Johnson, "Threats and Responses: The Overview. Reports That Led to Terror Alert Were Years Old, Officials Say," New York Times, 3 Aug. 2004, A1; Chaim F. Shatan, "Bogus Manhood, Bogus Honor: Surrender and Transfiguration in the United States Marine Corps," The Psychoanalytic Review (Winter 1977): 600;

Richard Goldstein, "Neo-Macho Man: Pop Culture and Post-9/11 Politics," The Nation, 24 March 2003, 16. Later in August 2004, Arnold Schwarzenegger, governor of California, did not hesitate to publicly ridicule Democratic politicians as "girlie men" to the wild applause of the assembled delegates of the Republican national convention in New York.

23 Corey Robin, *Fear: The History of a Political Idea* (Oxford, 2004), 155-58; Jane Mayer, *The Dark Side: The Inside Story of How the War on Terror Turned into a War on American Ideals* (Doubleday, 2008), 196; Mark Danner, *Torture and Truth: America, Abu Ghraib, and the War on Terror* (New York Review of Books, 2004). In a sense, it was if private TV viewers and the media took back the right over life and death once held by the old punitive sovereignty, which, according to the seventeenth-century English political philosopher Hobbes, had mythically been handed over to the absolute sovereign in exchange for civil peace and protection; in the U.S. this reassertion of the ancient right arguably began in the 1970s with the reinstatement of the death penalty (now commonly viewed as barbaric by the international community), in which the state served as the instrument of personal vengeance of grieving families and afflicted communities. See Giorgio Agamben, *Homo Sacer: Sovereign Power and Bare Life* (Stanford, 1998), 106; Butler, *Precarious Life*, 50-100; Adam Thurschwell, "Ethical Exception: Capital Punishment in the Figure of Sovereignty," *South Atlantic Quarterly* 107.3 (July 2008): 571-96; on the distinct concepts of revenge in traditional and modern societies, see Marcel Hénaff, "Global Terror, Global Vengeance?" *SubStance* 37.1 (2008): 72-97.

24 George Lakoff, *The Political Mind: Why You Can't Understand 21st-Century American Politics with an 18th-Century Brain* (Viking Penguin, 2008), 145-58; see also his *Don't Think of an Elephant!* (Chelsea Green Publications, 2005); Matt Bai, "The Framing Wars," *New York Times Magazine*, 17 July 2005.

http://www.nytimes.com/2005/07/17/magazine/the-framing-wars.html. Accessed 20 Feb. 2017.

25 Masha Gessen, "The Reichstag Fire Next Time: The Coming Crackdown," *Harper's Magazine*, 1 July 2017. https://harpers.org/archive/2017/07/the-reichstag-fire-next-time/. Accessed 2 July 2017.

26 Kate Zernike, "Kerry Pressing Swift Boat Case Long after Loss," *New York Times*, 28 May 2008: A1. http://www.nytimes.com/2006/05/28/washington/28kerry.html. Accessed 20 Feb. 2017.

27 Lakoff, *The Political Mind*, 13-14. For a complementary analysis of linguistic vulnerability, the performative force of language, and the sovereign power attributed to hate speech, see Judith Butler, *Excitable Speech: A Politics of the Performative* (Routledge, 1997), 1-41, 72-82. On countering Trump's lies and misrepresentations as a misguided strategy, see Patrick Seymour, "The Case against 'Exposing' Fascists," *Lenin's Tomb* 19 Feb. 2017. http://www.leninology.co.uk/2017/02/the-case-against-exposing-fascists.html#disqus_thread. Accessed 3 March 2017.

28 Massumi, *Ontopower*, 194-96.

29 Bob Herbert, "Bullying the Homeless," *New York Times*, 29 Nov. 1999, A25; Wayne Barrett, *Rudy! An Investigative Biography of Rudolph Giuliani* (Basic Books, 2000). There is a dark side to New York City politics that existed throughout the twentieth century and included groups with strong affinities to European fascism and U.S. nativism; see Pearlstein, "I Thought I understood the American Right. Trump Proved Me Wrong."

30 Michael Powell and Russ Buettner, "In Matters Big and Small, Crossing Giuliani Had a Price," *New York Times*, 22 Jan. 2008. http://www.nytimes.com/2008/01/22/us/politics/22giuliani.html. Accessed 20 Feb. 2017.

31 But the sheen would soon wear off: later revelations concerning the Giuliani administration's failure to replace defective police and firemen's radios before 9/11 and to issue proper protective gear against toxic dust to emergency and cleanup workers toiling in the World Trade Center ruins, which cost hundreds of lives and left many others with chronic illnesses, would put an end to his career. Already, prior to 9/11, Giuliani had tried to revive his flagging political fortunes in an unsuccessful 2000 bid to run against Hillary Clinton for a Senate seat.

Much later, in 2016, he made another attempt at a comeback when he served as a campaign advisor to Donald Trump and encouraged rogue FBI agents in the New York office to put pressure on then FBI Director James Comey to break protocol and revive public doubts about Clinton's email server at the close of the presidential campaign, arguably contributing to her defeat.

32 Corey Robin, *Fear: The History of a Political Idea* (2004), 228; "Workplace Bullying: The Silent Epidemic," Editorial, *British Medical Journal* 326 (12 April 2003): 776-777.

33 In this fashion do bullies and violent aggressors seek to dominate: by creating weak subjects through demonstrating their targets' "injurability," as philosopher Judith Butler would say, and, in turn, by projecting themselves as sovereign subjects who are "impermeable to violence." This can be true of entire nations as much as it is for individuals and groups (Judith Butler, *Frames of War* [Verso, 2009], 47, 178-79). Often, this experience of demeaning violence forces victims into a state of self-loathing, or at least self-doubt, and they remain in perpetual fear of potential psychological or physical assaults. And if, like today in the U.S., this takes place in the context of a resurgence of public acts of violent personal and group sovereignty in daily life and politics at the expense of the sovereignty of others, it can convert the experience of unwanted acts of violence into a one of a permanent sense of abject subjecthood, unless it is countered by successful acts of

defiance and resistance of the kind that we have been witnessing since Trump's inauguration.

34 Brian Massumi, "The Future Birth of The Affective Fact: The Political Ontology of Threat" in *Ontopower: War, Powers, and the State of Exception* (Duke, 2015), 189-205.

35 Richard Goldstein, "The Faggot Factor: The Chickens Come Home to Roost at Columbine High," *Village Voice*, 5-11 May 1999; Human Rights Watch, *Hatred in the Hallways: Violence, Discrimination, against Lesbian, Gay, Bisexual, and Transgender Students in U.S. Schools* (Human Rights Watch, 2001); Bob Herbert, "A Volatile Young Man, Humiliation, and a Gun," *New York Times*, 19 April 2007, A27; Jessie Klein, *The Bully Society: School Shootings and the Crisis of Bullying in America's Schools* (New York University Press, 2012). Luckily today, thanks to the passionate mobilization of citizens against the Trump and Republican agenda, that sense of isolation and despair has not overwhelmed opponents of the current administration.

36 To stabilize ailing lending institutions and boost their profit margins the Federal Reserve increased by two points the interest rate spread between the rate at which banks themselves could borrow funds and the rate at which they could make loans to clients. This increased spread, or profit margin, remained in place years after it served its function and was testimony to the ascendency of the financial sector.

37 Wages, adjusted for inflation, would be twice what they are now. See Stan Sorscher, "We All Do Better When We All Do Better," *The Huffington Post*, 3 July 2012. http://www.huffingtonpost.com/stan-sorscher/we-all-do-better-when-we-all-do-better_b_1469635.html. Accessed Aug. 30, 2017.

38 Steve Keen, *Debunking Economics: The Naked Emperor Dethroned?* (Zed Books, 2011), 326-56, 395.

39 Simon Johnson, "The Quiet Coup," *Atlantic Magazine*, May 2009. Johnson is former Chief Economist of the IMF. https://www.theatlantic.com/magazine/archive/2009/05/th

e-quiet-coup/307364/. Accessed 28 July 2017; "Wall Street," *Wikipedia.* https://en.wikipedia.org/wiki/Wall_Street#In_the_New_York_economy. Accessed 9 July 2017.

40 Stanley Bing, *Crazy Bosses: Spotting Them, Serving Them, Surviving Them,* 1st edition (William Morrow, 1992), 59-70. This is the most succinct chronicle of the managerial revolution in the age of financialization. Bing is the pen name for Gil Schwartz, a columnist for *Fortune* magazine. Donald Trump surfed the surge in speculative investment and was an early user of corporate junk bonds to finance his $1.2 billion Taj Mahal casino in Atlantic City in 1988. The parent company Trump Entertainment Resorts eventually went bankrupt and was acquired by Carl Icahn in 2016. In March 2017 Florida's Seminole Indians purchased the casino for a pittance; Associated Press, "Trump Taj Mahal Casino Sold for 4 Cents on the Dollar, *Los Angeles Times,* 9 May 2017 http://www.latimes.com/business/la-fi-trump-taj-mahal-20170509-story.html. Accessed 15 July 2017.

41 Judy Wajcman, "Desperately Seeking Differences: Is Management Style Gendered?" *British Journal of Industrial Relations* 34.3: 345.

42 Hugh D. Menzies, "The Ten Toughest Bosses." *Fortune,* 21 April 1980, 62-72; Peter Nulty and Karen Nickel, "America's Toughest Bosses," *Fortune,* 27 Feb. 1989, 40-46.

43 Nulty and Nickel, "America's Toughest Bosses"; John A. Byrne, "Chainsaw," *Business Week,* 18 Oct. 1999, 128-38.

44 Bing, *Crazy Bosses,* 103.

45 Brian Dumaine, "America's Toughest Bosses," *Fortune,* 18 Oct. 1993, 38-46.

46 Gina Vega and Debra R. Comer, "Sticks and Stones May Break Your Bones, but Words Can Break Your Spirit: Bullying in the Workplace," *Journal of Business Ethics* 58 (2005): 101-109.

47 Wajcman, "Desperately Seeking Differences," 344. This is a good example of what sociologists Charles Derber and Yale Magrass call "structural bullying" practiced by institutions: see their *Bully Nation: How the American Establishment Creates a Bullying Society* (University Press of Kansas, 2016), 7. On the deterioration of the workplace environment, see Richard Sennett, *The Corrosion of Character: The Personal Consequences of Work in the New Capitalism* (Norton, 1998) and Barbara Enrenreich's lively accounts of working under the new managerial practices, *Nickel and Dimed: On (Not) Getting By in America* (Picador, 2001) and *Bait and Switch: The (Futile) Pursuit of the American Dream* (Holt, 2006); see also Harvey Hornstein, *Brutal Bosses and Their Prey* (Riverhead, 1997).

A helpful a summary of abusive practices in the contemporary American workplace that reach even into employees' private life can be found in political philosopher Elizabeth Anderson, *Private Government: How Employers Rule Our Lives (and Why We Don't Talk about It* (Princeton, 2017), 38, 55-64. She deems the modern firm a form of "private government... that has arbitrary, unaccountable power over those it governs" (45), and its structure of centralized authority, a "communist dictatorship" (37-39). For a detailed analysis of psychological intimidation and bullying, see the French psychiatrist Marie-France Hirigoyen's accessible book that changed French workplace law, *Stalking the Soul: Emotional Abuse and the Erosion of Identity* (Helen Marx Books, 2000). On ordinary or "social" suffering as a fundamental experience in contemporary daily life, more academically inclined readers will want to consult German social philosopher Axel Honneth, *Disrespect: The Normative Foundations of Critical Theory* (Polity Press, 2007).

48 Cited in Bing, *Crazy Bosses,* 72, 85; C. Wright Mills, *The Power Elite* (Oxford, 1956), 361.

49 Richard C. Grote. *Forced Ranking: Making Performance Management Work.* (Harvard Business School, 2005).

[50] Deborah Lee, "An Analysis of Workplace Bullying in the UK," *Personnel Review* 29.5 (2000): 599-600; Leah Larkin, "Europe Dodges Tough Laws by Bullying Staff out of Jobs," *Personnel Today*, 2 Aug. 2005.

[51] Joel H. Neuman and Robert A. Baron, "Workplace Violence and Workplace Aggression: Evidence Concerning Specific Forms, Potential Causes, and Preferred Targets," *Journal of Management* 24.3 (1998): 391-409.

[52] Wim Vanderkerckhove and M.S. Ronald Commers, "Downward Workplace Mobbing: A Sign of the Times," *Journal of Business Ethics* 45 (2003): 41-50.

[53] Bing, *Crazy Bosses*, 100-101.

[54] At least until the advent of Obama's Affordable Care Act in 2010, which loosened the ties between employment and access to quality health insurance, thus diminishing leverage management historically enjoyed over recalcitrant employees (which perhaps goes a long way to explaining the vehement opposition to the ACA by many private employers). The "at-will employment" regime has undergone several changes at the state level, where some protection has been granted against unchecked firings. See Charles J. Muhl, "The Employment-At-Will Doctrine: Three Major Exceptions," *Monthly Labor Review* (Jan. 2001): 3-11.

[55] David Gordon, *Fat and Mean: The Corporate Squeeze of Working Americans and the Myth of Managerial "Downsizing,"* (Free Press, 1996).

[56] Susan Jeffords, *The Remasculinization of America: Gender and the Vietnam War* (Indiana, 1989) and *Hard Bodies: Hollywood Masculinity in the Reagan Era* (Rutgers, 1994); Susan Faludi, *Stiffed: The Betrayal of the American Man* (William Morrow, 1999).

[57] See Carol Anderson, *White Rage: The Unspoken Truth of Our Racial Divide* (Bloomsbury, 2016).

[58] It's worth noting that long before 2011, when he assumed the mantle of chief proponent of "birtherism," which

questioned Barack Obama's nationality, Trump's first attention-getting political act was to publish a sensationalist open letter in the form of full-page ads in all four New York City major dailies before the Central Park Jogger case went to trial, calling for the return of the death penalty and the execution of the five accused young men with the headlines, "Bring Back the Death Penalty" and "Bring Back Our Police!" and in which he trumpeted his hatred of violent criminals. Years later, in 2001, the youths' convictions were vacated after an investigation revealed that their confessions had been obtained under torture while in police custody and that the confession of a convicted rapist had been confirmed through DNA testing.

In 2014 New York City settled with the wrongfully convicted men for $40 million, which an unrepentant Trump denounced as "a disgrace." See "Donald Trump: Central Park Five Settlement a Disgrace," *New York Daily News* 21 June 2014. http://www.nydailynews.com/new-york/nyc-crime/donald-trump-central-park-settlement-disgrace-article-1.1838467. Accessed 10 July 2017. As Rick Pearlstein writes, Trump's call for execution regardless of evidence "mimics the rituals of Southern lynchings"; Rick Pearlstein, "I Thought I Understood the American Right. Trump Proved Me Wrong," *New York Times Magazine* 11 April 2017. https://www.nytimes.com/2017/04/11/magazine/i-thought-i-understood-the-american-right-trump-proved-me-wrong.html?smid=fb-share&_r=0. Accessed 30 April 2017.

59 Ishmael Reed, *Mixing It Up: Taking on the Media Bullies and Other Reflections* (Da Capo Press, 2008); Michelle Alexander, *The New Jim Crow: Mass Incarceration in the Age of Color-Blindness* (New Press, 2010), 189.

60 The culture wars that convulsed U.S. educational and cultural institutions (1985-1999) involved struggles over definitions of national culture, U.S. history, civil and sexual rights, artistic freedom and censorship, HIV/AIDS prevention campaigns, affirmative action, laws targeting discrimination and harassment in the workplace, and the material

protections afforded by the welfare state. They were an early proving ground for conservative smears of opponents, in this case, proponents of multiculturalism, feminism, anti-foundational French philosophy, and "political correctness." See Roddey Reid, "Foucault in America: Biography, 'Culture War', and the New Consensus," *Cultural Critique* (Winter/Spring 1997): 179-211.

[61] "The Arrival of Shouting Heads: The 'Argument Culture' in TV's Talk Shows Drives out Thoughtful Debate," Editorial, *Columbia Journalism Review* (Nov.-Dec. 2001): 122.

[62] Eric Alterman, *Sound and Fury: The Making of the Punditocracy* (Cornell, 1999).

[63] On the power of modern glamour and the promise of self-transformation it extends to mass audiences in democratic societies, see Stephen Gundle, *Glamour: A History* (Oxford, 2008) and Jackie Stacey, *Star Gazing: Hollywood Cinema and Female Spectatorship* (Routledge, 1994).

[64] Yehuda Baruch, "Bullying on the Net: Adverse Behavior on Email and Its Impact," *Information & Management* 42.2 (Jan. 2005): 361-371; Bob Tedeschi, "After Suicide, Blog Insults Are Debated," *New York Times*, 3 March 2008; Jesse McKinley, "Suicides Put Light on Pressures of Gay Teenagers," *New York Times*, 3 October 2010.

[65] David Yamada, "The Phenomenon of 'Workplace Bullying' and the Need for Status-Blind Hostile Work Environment Protection," *Georgetown Law Journal* 88.3 (2000): 475-546.

[66] Stephen Brooks, "Hate Speech and the Rights Cultures of Canada and the United States," *49th Parallel: An Interdisciplinary Journal of North America Studies* 13 (Spring 2004).

[67] Donald Trump with Tony Schwartz, *Trump: The Art of the Deal* (Random House, 1987), 1; Quincy Troupe, "My Take," *Black Renaissance Noire* 15.2 (Fall 2015), 4. A very

brief version of this chapter was first posted to my personal blog, "UnSafe Thoughts," in July 2016.

[68] Political commentators took Trump's personality seriously but then trivialized it by reducing it to mere psychology, overlooking the fact that personal attributes are also socially rooted.

[69] Trump broke with the post–Civil Rights ethos of "racial indifference" that, according to Michelle Alexander, characterizes the new Jim Crow racial caste system that operates via the color-blind criminal justice system. Instead, he substitutes and legitimizes a return to public expression of racial hostility that reigned under the old Jim Crow laws and regulations; see Michelle Alexander, *The New Jim Crow* (New Press, 2010), 14. White supremacists and the alt.right were quick to recognize Trump for who he is.

[70] Michael Lewis, *Liar's Poker* (Norton, 1989). His daughter Ivanka is also a *cum laude* Wharton School graduate.

[71] In his announcement of his presidential bid Trump famously disputed *Forbes*'s estimate of his wealth in 2015 at $4.1 billion claiming that it omitted the value of his brand worth over $3 billion. See Erin Carlyle, "Trump Exaggerating His Net Worth (by 100%) in Presidential Bid," *Forbes* 16 June 2015. https://www.forbes.com/sites/erincarlyle/2015/06/16/trump -exaggerating-his-net-worth-by-100-in-presidential- bid/#69b087322a97. Accessed 27 June 2017. Naomi Klein is one of the few commentators to appreciate the true measure of Trump's entrepreneurial persona, though only after the election. See her *No Is Not Enough*, 15-34.

[72] William F. Buckley, "The Demagogues Are Running," *Cigar Aficionado* (March-April 2000). http://www.cigaraficionado.com/webfeatures/show?id=7081. Accessed 15 Aug. 2016; Samuel Francis, "From Household to Nation: The Middle American Populism of Pat Buchanan," *Chronicles* (March 1996): 12-17.

http://theweek.com/articles/599577/how-obscure-adviser-pat-buchanan-predicted-wild-trump-campaign-1996; http://www.unz.org/Pub/Chronicles-1996mar-00012. Accessed 8 Aug. 2016.

73 Gopnik writes from a reflexively antipopulist position that asserted that Donald Trump and Bernie Sanders both posed threats to liberal democracy: "The Dangerous Acceptance of Donald Trump," *New Yorker*, 20 May 2016. http://www.newyorker.com/news/daily-comment/the-dangerous-acceptance-of-donald-trump. Accessed 1 June 2016.

74 The same Manhattan-centric condescension was extended to Brooklyn-born candidate Bernie Sanders as well.

75 Frank Rich, "The Importance of Donald Trump," *New York Magazine*, 21 Sept.-4 Oct. 2015. http://nymag.com/daily/intelligencer/2015/09/frank-rich-in-praise-of-donald-trump.html. Accessed 15 Aug. 2017. Non-white and non-mainstream writers generally took Trump seriously early on; for example, see poet and *Black Renaissance Noire* editor Quincy Troupe's column, "My Take," 4-5.

76 Masha Gessen, "Masha Gessen on Truth, Lies, and Totalitarianism in Russia and the U.S.," Bay Area Book Festival, 3 June 2017. On contemporary populist movements, see John B. Judis, *The Populist Explosion: How the Great Recession Transformed American and European Politics* (Columbia Global Reports, 2016).

77 Political commentators across the ideological spectrum decried Trump's campaign speeches and State of the Union speech, written by alt.right advisor Steve Bannon, bemoaning American decline for breaking with the quasi-sacred political American tradition of political optimism. What they failed to understand is that in so doing, Trump concentrated voters' hopes and aspirations *on his very person*, converting himself into what writer Christopher Brown calls the "savior CEO"; see Christopher Brown, "You're Fired: Democracy, Dystopia

and the Cult of the CEO," *Shift Newco*, 15 March 2017. https://shift.newco.co/youre-fired-democracy-dystopia-and-the-cult-of-the-ceo-83a3a9b24531#.labya7uxj. Accessed 20 March 2017.

[78] Brian Massumi, *The Power at the End of the Economy* (Duke, 2015), 6. Italics in the original. In a parallel fashion, sociologist Charles Thorpe resurrects German psychoanalyst Erich Fromm's use of the concept of "negative freedom" to trace the violent dynamic at the heart of libertarianism between greater "freedom" from others and the resulting experience of growing insecurity; see "The Tyranny of Negative Freedom" in *Necroculture* (Palgrave Macmillan, 2016), 205-59.

[79] Robert O. Paxton, "The Five Stages of Fascism," *Journal of Modern History*, 70.1 (March 1998): 1-23.

[80] In truth, the violent assertion of individual and group sovereignty at the expense of others is as old as the nation itself, starting with the European conquest and settlement of the continent. The democratic promise of America was always one of offering the possibility of being one's own master but, as Corey Robin reminds us, in the conservative version, also the promise of being the master of others (in the case of white men, the opportunity to own slaves); in this case one's freedom almost presupposes the domination and subjection of others; see his "Out of Place: Conservatives and the American Right," *The Nation*, 23 June 2008. https://www.thenation.com/article/out-place-0/. Accessed 20 June 2017. The massive incarceration of men of color over the last thirty years and their consequent social and economic disenfranchisement is the most brutal example of the return of violent, punitive sovereignty in daily life.

[81] Jamie C. Lee and Kevin Quealy, "The 342 People, Places, and Things Donald Trump Has Insulted on Twitter: A Complete List," *New York Times*, 18 July 2017. https://www.nytimes.com/interactive/2016/01/28/upshot/donald-trump-twitter-insults.html?smid=fb-

nytimes&smtyp=cur&_r=0#the-letter-B. Accessed 21 July 2017.

[82] Nick Corsanti and Maggie Haberman, "Trump Suggests That 'Second Amendment People' Could Act against Hillary Clinton," *New York Times*, 9. Aug. 2016. https://www.nytimes.com/2016/08/10/us/politics/donald-trump-hillary-clinton.html?_r=0. Accessed 25 Feb. 2017.

[83] Paxton, "The Five Stages of Fascism," 15-16. Thus for example, Trump can present himself as the embodiment of the promise of free-market capitalism, an opponent of globalization and the off-shoring of jobs, and an advocate of a renewed protectionism. It is not a principled position but rather *a politically effective one* popular with his base that fiercely defends the prerogatives of U.S. free markets against those of other countries: we can enter your markets with our goods but you can't enter ours. A nationalist, imperial free-market ideology of sorts, not unlike that of Great Britain in the nineteenth century.

As Karl Marx was fond of pointing out, behind every ambitious businessman who supports open competition and free trade also lurks an aspiring monopolist and protectionist. Pragmatic businessmen and politicians are disconcerting, for they can sail right through conceptual incoherence or intellectual contradictions that political philosophers and intellectual historians view as fatal to organizations and political movements.

[84] On the U.S. "working class" and their resentment towards the poor and successful professionals and their admiration of the rich, see Joan C. Williams, "What So Many People Don't Get about the U.S. Working Class," *Harvard Business Review*, 10 Nov. 2016. https://hbr.org/2016/11/what-so-many-people-dont-get-about-the-u-s-working-class. Accessed 28 August 2017. Thanks to Jerome Karabel for the reference.

[85] A word about glitz and glamour: they must be understood as a system rather than simply personal

attributes. According to Stephen Gundle, glamour in modern democratic mass societies has "contained the promise of mobile and commercial society that anyone could be transformed into a better, more attractive, wealthier version of themselves" as well as "opportunities... for self-invention and affirmation." That is the basis of its power of fascination.

By the same token, modern glamour has always been an unstable combination of success, wealth, and fame with more than a whiff of notoriety and illegitimacy. It is a "mix of class and sleaze" in which social mobility is assumed to be the product of talent, luck, unethical arrangements, and in the case of women, sexual favors (Gundle, *Glamour*, 7-17, 34). Illegitimacy alludes to the humble origins of most celebrities and asks the cynical question of how they achieved their exalted status, while bad behavior is the mark of freedom celebrities enjoy that ordinary citizens can only dream of and willingly tolerate in their idols.

Like his real estate career, Trump's vulgar ostentation and excess goes back to the go-go 1980s, and is the contemporary tabloid version of glamour. With great success, he has converted one of glamour's functions as a "safety valve of social impulses" back into an aggressive weapon that exploits for social and political ends those very same desires, fears, and anxieties of voters, from which glamour is meant to serve as a distraction.

86 Corey Pein, "Mouthbreathing Machiavelli's Dream of a Silicon Reich," *The Baffler*, 19 May 2014. http://thebaffler.com/blog/mouthbreathing-machiavellis#. Accessed 15 Feb. 2017. Pein's article offers useful background to the libertarian universe of tech bloggers and executives whose thinking echoes neoreactionary writers such as Mencius Moldbug (Curtis Guy Yarvin), Nick Land, and Lawrence Auster. Their positions are close to those of the alt-right.

Best known to the general public is PayPal cofounder, hedge fund manager, and Trump supporter Peter Thiel, who has gone beyond mainstream libertarianism to declare freedom and democracy as incompatible and advocated for the monarchical structure of start-ups as a model of political rule. Less known is Balaji Srinivasan, cofounder of genomic start-up company Counsyl, who promotes autonomous corporate city-states as the future of government. For a broader look at political philosophies popular in the tech industry, see Julianne Tveten and Paul Blest, "Silicon Valley Won't Save You," *Current Affairs* 31 July 2017. https://www.currentaffairs.org/2017/07/silicon-valley-wont-save-you. Accessed 9 August 2107. On CEOs' desire to follow Trump to the White House, see James B. Stewart, "With Trump in the White House, Some Executives Ask, Why Not Me?" *New York Times*, 9 March 2017. https://www.nytimes.com/2017/03/09/business/bloomberg-iger-business-executives-president.html. Accessed 13 July 2017.

87 To be fair, Dean went on the become chair of the Democratic Party 's governing body, the Democratic National Committee, where he launched an innovative fifty-state strategy that won additional congressional seats for the party in 2006 and 2008. This renewed commitment to more local politics would not last the advent of Obama's presidency, however. For more on Obama's 2008 campaign and first administration, see below.

88 Kim Phillips-Fein, *Invisible Hands: The Businessmen's Crusade Against the New Deal* (Norton, 2010).

89 It is worth noting that a careful review of Obama's 2009 Inaugural Address reveals that Obama held all political factions and their respective political doctrines equally responsible for the harsh political climate, as in the following sentence: "On this day, we gather because we have chosen hope over fear, unity of purpose over conflict and discord. On this day, we come to proclaim an end to petty grievances and false promises, the recriminations and worn-out dogmas that for too long have strangled our politics." ("President Barack Obama's Inaugural Address," the White House, 21 January

2009
https://obamawhitehouse.archives.gov/blog/2009/01/21/pre
sident-barack-obamas-inaugural-address. Accessed 20 July
2017).

As practiced by Democratic leaders like Obama, such an
even-handed, bipartisan approach meant to calm the public is
simply not equipped to deal with the roots and causes of
contemporary political violence.

90 It is also a reminder that in the United States, unlike
most industrialized countries, federal and state governments
never fully achieved a monopoly of armed violence, which is
one of the hallmarks of the modern nation-state. "Man Carries
Assault Rifle to Obama Protest—and It's Legal," *Time*, 18 Aug.
2009.
http://www.cnn.com/2009/POLITICS/08/17/obama.protest.
rifle/. Accessed 15 Feb. 2017. Scott Horsley, "Guns by the
Numbers," *NPR*, 5 Jan. 2016.
http://www.npr.org/2016/01/05/462017461/guns-in-
america-by-the-numbers. Accessed 27 Feb. 2017.

The National Rifle Association's video released in July
2017 that is riddled with hatred of Jews and Blacks and
threatened Trump's opponents with violence from its own
members should dispel any illusions about the political
purpose of its mission.
https://www.nratv.com/series/freedoms-safest-
place/episode/freedoms-safest-place-season-2-episode-2-the-
violence-of-lies. Accessed 15 July 2017. Black Lives Matter,
displaying a mastery of quick response countering slander
within the same news cycle, issued a powerful video
demanding that the NRA retract the inflammatory video:
https://www.youtube.com/watch?v=7B7MUceV2og&oref=htt
ps%3A%2F%2Fwww.youtube.com%2Fwatch%3Fv%3D7B7M
UceV2og&has_verified=1.

91 Jonathan Raban, "Gabrielle Giffords is the Victim of a
Debased Political Culture," *The Independent*, 21 Jan. 2011.
http://www.independent.co.uk/news/world/americas/gabriel

le-giffords-is-the-victim-of-a-debased-political-culture-2180268.html Accessed 21 Feb. 2017; Sandhya Somashekhar, "Sheriff Dupnik's Criticism of Political 'Vitriol' Resonates with the Public," *Washington Post*, 9 Jan. 2011. http://voices.washingtonpost.com/44/2011/01/sheriff-dupniks-criticism-of-p.html. Accessed 2 March 2017; Michael Martinez, "Shooting Throws Spotlight on State of U.S. Political Rhetoric," *CNN*, 10 Jan. 2011. http://www.cnn.com/2011/US/01/09/arizona.shooting.rhetoric/index.html. Accessed 2 March 2017.

When in the wake of massive public protests against the new Trump administration, the vast majority of Republicans refused to hold the traditional town halls with constituents during the February 2016 congressional recess, former Congresswoman Giffords issued a press release mocking them for their cowardice reminding them that her congressional office continued to hold public meetings after the 2011 attack: http://americansforresponsiblesolutions.org/2017/02/23/townhall/. Accessed 3 March 2017.

92 Roger D. Hodge, *The Mendacity of Hope* (HarperCollins, 2010). Overlooked by many Obama supporters during the campaign was the fact that Obama had called for escalating the Afghan War and that his biggest campaign donors came from Wall Street; their money dwarfed the record contributions of his many small donors. See David Dayen, "The Most Important WikiLeaks Revelation Isn't About Hillary Clinton. What John Podesta's Emails from 2008 Reveal about the Way Power Works in the Democratic Party," *The New Republic*, 14 Oct. 2016:

> Michael Froman, who is now U.S. trade representative but at the time was an executive at Citigroup, wrote an email to Podesta on October 6, 2008, with the subject "Lists." Froman used a Citigroup email address. He attached three documents: a list of women for top administration

jobs, a list of non-white candidates, and a sample outline of 31 cabinet-level positions and who would fill them. 'The lists will continue to grow,' Froman wrote to Podesta, 'but these are the names to date that seem to be coming up as recommended by various sources for senior level jobs.'

The cabinet list ended up being almost entirely on the money. It correctly identified Eric Holder for the Justice Department, Janet Napolitano for Homeland Security, Robert Gates for Defense, Rahm Emanuel for chief of staff, Peter Orszag for the Office of Management and Budget, Arne Duncan for Education, Eric Shinseki for Veterans Affairs, Kathleen Sebelius for Health and Human Services, Melody Barnes for the Domestic Policy Council, and more. For the Treasury, three possibilities were on the list: Robert Rubin, Larry Summers, and Timothy Geithner.

https://newrepublic.com/article/137798/important-wikileaks-revelation-isnt-hillary-clinton. Accessed 3 March 2017.

93 According to David Bromwich, this constituted a recurring pattern in the course of Obama's career; he quickly adapted his views and goals to the institutions and organizations that he joined: "The Character of Barack Obama," *Huffington Post*, 4 Sept. 2009. http://www.huffingtonpost.com/david-bromwich/character-of-barack-obama_b_251186.html. Accessed 20 Feb. 2017. See also his "What Went Wrong: Assessing Obama's Legacy," *Harper's Magazine*, June 2015. http://harpers.org/archive/2015/06/what-went-wrong/. Accessed 3 March 2017.

94 Micah Sifry, "Obama's Lost Army," *The New Republic*, 9 February 2017.

https://newrepublic.com/article/140245/obamas-lost-army-inside-fall-grassroots-machine. Accessed 20 July 2017.

95 It is interesting to note that Democratic presidential candidates most adept at hardball politics have had the closest ties to local political machines. One thinks of John F. Kennedy (Irish-American organizations in Boston and Chicago) and Lyndon Baines Johnson and Bill Clinton (state politics in the Deep South). Unlike fellow Chicagoan Rahm Emmanuel, Obama does not seem to have absorbed those lessons, but in neither case did Obama or Emmanuel apply them in their dealings with Republicans in Washington. They saved them largely for intraparty squabbles.

96 Much like today and in 1995 , in 1953 once they won control of both the White House and Congress, they redoubled their efforts of intimidation with little apparent concern for possible political consequences for themselves.

97 During his reelection campaign in 1996, in an appeal to the aspirational ethos of his base, Bill Clinton made a central theme of "playing by the rules" and hard work (but not entrepreneurialism as such) as the promise of an equal opportunity society; it was something which he preached but in the event obviously did not practice. Realizing the American Dream (especially for immigrants) has been the fundamental political promise of Democratic Party for the last thirty years.

98 Carl Freedman (personal communication).

99 Judicial Watch, a conservative non-profit think-tank that filed the successful Freedom of Information Act request for Clinton's emails has been investigating the Clintons for twenty-years in search of scandal, generating many defaming headlines.

100 Shankar Subramaniam (personal communication).

101 Roddey Reid, "The American Culture of Public Bullying," *Black Renaissance Noire* 10.2-3 (Fall–Winter 2009-10): 175.

[102] For a succinct synopsis of the elections, see Jerome Karabel, "The Roots of the Democratic Debacle," *Huffington Post*, 12 Dec. 2016. http://www.huffingtonpost.com/entry/the-roots-of-the-democratic-debacle_us_584ec983e4b04c8e2bb0a779. Accessed 15 Dec. 2016.

[103] Instead of disqualifying ballots, as they did in 2000, Republicans in 2016 succeeded in disqualifying voters pure and simple—as many as 300,000 in Wisconsin alone, which Trump carried by a mere margin of 23,000 votes.

[104] For Trump's emergence as a CEO populist candidate, see Chapter Three; for an excellent overview of the "savior CEO," see Christopher Brown, "You're Fired: Democracy, Dystopia and the Cult of the CEO," *Shift Newco*, 15 March 2017. https://shift.newco.co/youre-fired-democracy-dystopia-and-the-cult-of-the-ceo-83a3a9b24531#.labya7uxj. Accessed 20 March 2017.

[105] See Alexander Stille, "Donald Trump, America's Own Silvio Berlusconi," *The Intercept*, 7 March 2016. https://theintercept.com/2016/03/07/what-the-past-of-silvio-berlusconi-tells-us-about-the-future-of-donald-trump/. Accessed 23 Feb. 2017; and also Stille, *The Sack of Rome: How a Beautiful European Country with a Fabled History and Storied Culture Was Taken Over by a Man Named Silvio Berlusconi* (Penguin, 2006). The 2007 paperback edition carries a more succinct subtitle, *Media + Money + Celebrity = Power = Berlusconi*. Like Trump, Berlusconi was the product of the old system but presented himself as a fresh alternative; and like Trump he got his start in shady real estate dealings.

However, as Stille is careful to point out, the comparison works only so far: Berlusconi soon parlayed his early business successes into a matchless media empire that gave him a monopoly of Italian television and made him Italy's richest man, something Trump can only dream of. He even created his own political party, named after the Milan football team he owns, *Forza Italia*, and, filled with his own executives, managers, and employees, it became an unheralded patronage machine.

Like Trump's followers, Berlusconi's were fed up with the traditional party politics (of the Italian Christian Democratic, Communist, and Socialist parties) but apparently they were much less ideological and less committed to particular political issues: "Berlusconi understood that voters were more interested in personality than programs, and what he needed to do was to sell himself and the lifestyle he represented" (163). During his terms of office Berlusconi presided over a steep decline in the economy's competitiveness, the weakening of its judiciary, and the provincialization of its foreign policy.

[106] Jonathan Mahler, "CNN Had a Problem. Donald Trump Solved It," *New York Times*, 4 April 2017 https://www.nytimes.com/2017/04/04/magazine/cnn-had-a-problem-donald-trump-solved-it.html?mcubz=1. Accessed 15 July 2017.

[107] Glenn Greenwald (interview), "Why Did Trump Win? Blame the Failed Policies of the Democratic Party," *Democracy Now!* 10 Nov. 2016 https://www.democracynow.org/2016/11/10/glenn_greenwal d_why_did_trump_win. Accessed 23 Feb. 2017.

[108] On the fatal role uncritical use of "big data" played in the Clinton campaign, see David Auerbach, "Confirmation Bias: Did Big Data Sink the Clinton Campaign?" *n+1*, 23 Feb. 2017. https://nplusonemag.com/online-only/online-only/confirmation-bias/. Accessed 28 Feb. 2017.

[109] But as political sociologist Mike Davis is careful to point out, Democrats performed poorly up and down the ballot, locally as well as nationally; the problem went beyond the Clinton campaign itself. Mike Davis, "The Great God Trump and the White Working Class," *Jacobin*, 7 Feb. 2017. https://www.jacobinmag.com/2017/02/the-great-god-trump-and-the-white-working-class/. Accessed 22 Feb. 2017.

[110] Steven Shaviro (personal communication).

[111] Nate Silver, "The Polls Missed Trump. We Asked Pollsters Why," *FiveThirtyEight*, 9 Nov. 2016. Accessed 20 Feb. 2017. https://fivethirtyeight.com/features/the-polls-missed-trump-we-asked-pollsters-why/. In later accounts Silver would discount the "Trump effect" on polling accuracy.

[112] For an early example of the *New York Times'* treatment of Bernie Sanders, see David Bromwich, "Bernie Sanders Gets Slimed by the *New York Times*," *Salon*, 6 July 2015. http://www.salon.com/2015/07/06/bernie_sanders_gets_sli med_by_the_new_york_times_this_is_what_a_smiling_co ndescending_hit_job_looks_like/. Of course, Clinton herself was not well treated by the mainstream media either, focused as they were on sensationalist coverage of her private email server, hacked email accounts, troubles with her staff, the Clinton Foundation's finances, and the Benghazi incident in Libya.

[113] One is struck also by the surprised reaction of Clinton, her supporters, and senior Democrats, including Obama, to the release of the hacked emails by Wikileaks founder Julian Assange. Since both Clinton and Obama had already sought to prosecute him for releasing secret documents detailing wanton killing by U.S. forces in Afghanistan, their expressed outrage at actions targeting them by someone they had helped turn into a powerful political enemy appears disingenuous at best, naïve at worst.

[114] In this fashion it goes beyond linguist George Lakoff's focus on the power of political messaging as primarily one of repetition and reinforcement.

[115] Wendy Brown, "American Nightmare: Neoliberalism, Neoconservatism, and De-Democratization," *Political Theory* 43.6 (Dec. 2006): 707-08.

[116] Brian Massumi, *Ontopower: War, Powers, And the State of Perception* (Duke, 2015), 267.

[117] A March 22, 2017 Quinnipiac Poll reported that subsequent to the Trump/Republican health care proposal to cut Medicaid benefits, Trump's support among Republicans

dropped 14 points from 95% to 81% in a mere two weeks. As of May 24, 2017 it stood at 84% despite all the turmoil in his administration and dropped further to 72% in late June. https://poll.qu.edu/national/release-detail?ReleaseID=2442. Accessed 25 May 2017; Esme Cribb, "Digits among GOPers since 100th Day," *Talking Points Memo*, 20 June, 2017. http://talkingpointsmemo.com/polltracker/trump-approval-down-among-republicans. Accessed 25 June 2017. It has remained steady overall ever since.

As mentioned previously, even after Trump's expression of sympathy for violent white supremacist and neo-Nazi demonstrators in Charlottesville, Virginia, he still enjoyed a 77% approval rating among Republicans according to the August 23 Quinnipiac University Poll. https://poll.qu.edu/national/release-detail?ReleaseID=2482. Accessed 26 August 2017.

[118] Arguably, it is not clear that Trump the tyrannical CEO is even interested in accumulating wealth per se but rather, ever the macho entrepreneur who is always on to the next business opportunity, he seems more focused on expanding his brand, cutting deals, and exercising power—and terror—over others. On Trump as a violent icon of capitalist culture legitimated by current workplace practices and media culture, see Chapter Three. For a brief history of the "CEO savior" and possible corporate transformations of the federal government see Christopher Brown, "You're Fired: Democracy, Dystopia, and the Cult of the CEO," *Shift Newco* 15 March 2015 https://shift.newco.co/youre-fired-democracy-dystopia-and-the-cult-of-the-ceo-83a3a9b24531#.r3pyqhmz4. Accessed 19 March 2017.

[119] After all, the Republicans are in charge of the White House, Congress, federal agencies, the Supreme Court, thirty-two statehouses, and thirty-one governorships. The entire federal judiciary may fall under their control if they succeed in filling over one hundred and twenty outstanding vacancies on the federal bench, especially at the appellate level.

[120] Daniel Marans, "Progressives Slam Tom Perez's New DNC Transition Team," *Huffington Post*, 16 March 2017. http://www.huffingtonpost.com/entry/progressives-tom-perez-dnc-transition-committee_us_58cab459e4boec9d29d9695f 16 March 2017. Accessed 17 March 2017.

[121] In terms of the mainstream media, the most egregious example was the publication by the *Washington Post* of a "blacklist" of 200 journalists, websites, and news organizations serving as Russian agents; see James Carden, "'The Washington Post' Promotes a McCarthyite Blacklist," *The Nation*, 28 Nov. 2016. https://www.thenation.com/article/the-washington-post-promotes-a-mccarthyite-blacklist/. Accessed 21 March 2017.

As of this writing (late July 2017), as investigations of Russian collusion proceed and Trump threatens to fire Attorney-General Jeff Sessions, the smearing of liberals and progressives who raise questions about available public evidence has taken on a new life; see Peter Beinart, "Trump's Defenders on the Left," *The Atlantic*, 23 July 2107 https://www.theatlantic.com/international/archive/2017/07/russia-trump-left/534534/. Accessed 26 July 2017; Jeet Heer, "Why the Anti-War Left Should Attack Putin, Too," *The New Republic*, 25 July 2017. https://newrepublic.com/article/144009/anti-war-left-attack-putin. Accessed 26 July 2017.

[122] Glenn Greenwald, "Democratic Tactics of Accusing Critics of Kremlin Allegiance Has a Long Ugly History in U.S.," *The Intercept*, 8 Aug. 2016. https://theintercept.com/2016/08/08/dems-tactic-of-accusing-adversaries-of-kremlin-ties-and-russia-sympathies-has-long-history-in-us/. Accessed 22 March 2017.

[123] Even Howard Dean, victim of political smears by Democratic leaders and tendentious reporting by the *New York Times* correspondents Jodi Wilgoren and Adam Nagourney during the 2004 primaries, as a fervent 2016

Clinton supporter engaged in a smear of his own in a Dec. 21, 2016 tweet speculating that *The Intercept* may be on the Russian payroll. https://twitter.com/govhowarddean/status/81160712602406 5028?lang=en. Accessed 25 Feb. 2017.

124 But not that of his chief counsel Roy Cohn, who retired to New York City, where he led a life of celebrity, served as attorney to unscrupulous politicians and businessmen, trafficked in political influence and intrigue, and later tutored his client Donald Trump in the dark arts of the smear. Nicholas von Hoffman, *Citizen Cohn: The Life and Times of Roy Cohn* (Doubleday: 1988), 237. The televised Army-McCarthy proceedings were the subject of a famous documentary film titled *Point of Order* (1964), by Emile de Antonio: https://www.youtube.com/watch?v=wJHsur3HqcI. The exchange between Joe Welch and McCarthy is captured here: https://www.youtube.com/watch?v=Po5GlFba5Yg. Accessed 2 April 2017.

125 Regarding how to respond to the intimidating tactics of far-right and alt.right groups that show up in your community, the Southern Poverty Law Center has offered two guides, one for college campuses, another for municipalities: "The Alt-Right and What Students Need to Know," 10 Aug. 2017. https://www.splcenter.org/news/2017/08/10/splc-releases-campus-guide-countering-%E2%80%98alt-right%E2%80%99; and a new edition of "Ten Ways to Fight Hate: A Community Response," 14 Aug. 2017. https://www.splcenter.org/20170814/ten-ways-fight-hate-community-response-guide. Accessed 30 Aug. 2017.

126 Becky Bond and Zack Exley, *Rules for Revolutionaries: How Big Organizing Can Change Everything* (Chelsea Green, 2017), 185-86.

127 Margaret Sullivan, "Jeff Zucker's Singular Role in Promoting Donald Trump's Rise," *Washington Post*, 2 Oct. 2016. https://www.washingtonpost.com/lifestyle/style/jeff-zuckers-singular-role-in-promoting-donald-trumps-

rise/2016/10/02/7c3d4366-865b-11e6-a3ef-f35afb41797f_story.html?utm_term=.80cbf8c13884. Accessed 15 July 2107; Glenn Greenwald (interview), "Why Did Trump Win? Blame the Failed Policies of the Democratic Party," *Democracy Now!* 10 Nov. 2016. https://www.democracynow.org/2016/11/10/glenn_greenwal d_why_did_trump_win. Accessed 23 Feb. 2017.

[128] Jonathan Mahler, "CNN Had a Problem. Donald Trump Solved It," *New York Times*, 4 April 2017. https://www.nytimes.com/2017/04/04/magazine/cnn-had-a-problem-donald-trump-solved-it.html?mcubz=1. Accessed 15 July 2017.

[129] *Indivisible: A Practical Guide for Resisting the Trump Agenda* (Updated 9 March 2017), 3; Judith Butler, "Survivability, Vulnerability, Affect," *Frames of War* (Verso, 2009), 48.

[130] This lesson was lost on the University of California, Berkeley administration in its dealings with local College Republicans, who had invited right-wing English provocateur Milo Yiannopoulos. Doubtless administrators thought they would avoid the ire of Washington by authorizing a campus speech in February 2017 by the *Breitbart News* editor— a known abuser of members of his public audiences— and by hewing to a broad interpretation of what constitutes "protected speech." They dismissed the substantive issue of Yiannopoulos's record of *conduct* (as opposed to his political opinions) of using a trigger camera to harass and incite others to harass transgender people present in the audience that concerned faculty brought to its attention.

The rest is history: anarchists rioted and damaged university property, the talk was cancelled, and Trump accused Berkeley of violating free speech and threatened it with the loss of federal funding. Predictably, Berkeley administrators got no credit for their misguided efforts to accommodate a known violent speaker. Six months later, *The Berkeley Patriot*, a conservative student newspaper, announced plans bring him back to campus with Ann Coulter and Steve Bannon in September 2017. Thomas Fuller and Christopher Mele, "Berkeley Cancels Milo Yiannopoulos Speech, And Donald Trump Tweets Outrage," *New York Times*, 1 Feb. 2017. https://www.nytimes.com/2017/02/01/us/uc-berkeley-milo-yiannopoulos-protest.html?mcubz=1&_r=0. Accessed 27 August 2017. https://twitter.com/realDonaldTrump/status/827112633224 544256?ref_src=twsrc%5Etfw. Accessed 14 March 2017.

[131] According to Nate Silver, from early March to late May *strong* approval of Trump's performance fell among Republicans from 29% to 21.4% but his overall approval rating remained the same. "Donald Trump's Base is Shrinking," *FiveThirtyEight*, 24 May 2017. https://fivethirtyeight.com/features/donald-trumps-base-is-shrinking/. Accessed 17 July 2017.

[132] Robert O. Paxton, *The Anatomy of Fascism* (Knopf, 2004), 148. Five months after Trump's election, Paxton decided that the fascist label does not apply to the new president. According to him, fascists generally advocate subordination of individual interests to the larger community and the state; they seek to strengthen government, not weaken it. Rather, Paxton views Trump as a potential generic dictator of sorts and a plutocrat in light of his social and economic libertarianism: "American Duce: Is Donald Trump a Fascist or a Plutocrat?" *Harper's Magazine* (May 2017), 38-39. https://harpers.org/archive/2017/05/american-duce/. Accessed 15 July 2017.

[133] For an interesting retrospective analysis of Occupy's strategic focus on centers of capitalist redistribution (e.g., the stock market) instead of production (workplaces) see Stephen Squibb, "What Was Occupy?" *Monthly Review* 66.9 (Feb. 2015). https://monthlyreview.org/2015/02/01/what-was-occupy/ Accessed 19 March 2017. He views its strategy as an attempt to capture and re-direct the "democratic" promise (if

not actuality) of redistribution of wealth symbolized by shareholder ownership under financialized capitalism.

134 When the Affordable Care Act passed in 2010, it provoked the violent opposition of white middle-class voters led by the libertarian Tea Party hostile to federal programs of any kind. The political irony is that before it was adopted by Democrats, it was originally a free market–based policy proposed by the conservative American Heritage Foundation and then implemented by Republican Governor Mitt Romney in Massachusetts, where it was a resounding success. It would appear that sponsorship at the federal level by our first black president discredited it in the eyes of many people. Moreover, the idea of allowing medical coverage to be extended to the over 40 million uninsured, who, in their minds, at least, are the undeserving poor (translate: people of color), was anathema to its opponents. Doubtless, for them, the new plan carried the same social stigma as the old U.S. welfare system.

To point out to them, as Democrats and liberal policymakers did, that in these difficult economic times they, too, may benefit one day from the advantages of a national health insurance system that covers every citizen and permanent resident seemed only to affront them. For to acknowledge and receive publicly such help would be tantamount not only to falling out of the great American middle class but also to joining voluntarily the ranks of people of color. In this view, "Better uninsured than no longer white." In 2017, the success of some of the key provisions of the ACA (allowing for preexisting conditions, new access for 18 million people to medical services, etc.), together with the prolonged public fight over Trumpcare, may have caused these attitudes to soften.

135*Democracy Now!* Philadelphia Free Library, 29 Nov. 2016 https://www.youtube.com/watch?v=2rEGCDR6wKQ. Accessed 21 March 2017.

82644653R00078